SOUNDARAYA INSTITUTE OF MANAGEMENT AND SCIENCE, BENGALURU

"INNOVATIONS IN BUSINESS PRACTICES: BRIDGING GLOBAL PERSPECTIVES" - 2025

Dr. Vasu B A

Prof. Vaibhav S Arwade

Dr. Roopa Shettigar

Prof. Angel Chakraborthy

Prof. Vasanth Kumar G

Prof. Vibin Krishnan R

ISBN
Hardcase 979-8-89961-797-3
Paperback 979-8-89961-798-0

Organising Committee

Dr. Vasu B A
Principal, Director, SIMS, Bengaluru.

Prof. Bhanu Prakash R
Assistant Professor, Department of MBA, SIMS

Prof. Yuvaraj Halage,
HoD & Assistant Professor, Department of MBA, SIMS

Advisory Committee

Mr. Muralidhar,
Founder, Loadster

Dr. Ravindra Babu Satya Narayana,
Professor, SBM, Christ University.

Dr. Bhavani M R,
Chanaakya University.

Message from Chairman's Desk…

Chairman's Desk Message

It is with great pride and pleasure that I welcome you to the International Conference on *"Innovations in Business Practices: Bridging Global Perspectives"* – 23rd March 2025, organized by the Department of MBA and BBA. In today's rapidly evolving global landscape, innovation is the driving force behind sustainable business growth and competitiveness. This conference serves as a vital platform for academicians, researchers, industry leaders, and students to share knowledge, exchange ideas, and build global partnerships.

The Book of Abstracts is a reflection of diverse thoughts, creative solutions, and progressive research that address contemporary challenges in business practices. Each contribution highlights the spirit of inquiry and innovation that our academic community fosters.

I extend my sincere gratitude to all participants, authors, reviewers, and the organizing team for their unwavering commitment. I am confident that this conference will inspire new perspectives and lasting collaborations.

Wishing you all a successful and enriching experience!

Warm regards,

Sri. Soundarya P Manjappa
Chairman
Soundarya Education Trust
Bengaluru Karnataka.

CEO's Message

It is with great pride that I welcome you to the International Conference on *"Innovations in Business Practices: Bridging Global Perspectives"* on this momentous day, March 23rd, 2025. This conference is a platform where global minds converge to exchange transformative ideas and shape the future of business. The Book of Abstracts reflects the depth and diversity of thought presented here. I wish all participants a meaningful, insightful, and inspiring journey of learning and collaboration.

Warm regards,

Mr. Keerthan Kumar M
Chief Executive Officer
Soundarya Education Trust
Bengaluru Karnataka.

Principal's/Director's Desk Message…

It gives me immense pleasure to welcome all participants to the International Conference on *"Innovations in Business Practices: Bridging Global Perspectives"* held on 23rd March 2025. In a rapidly evolving world, innovation serves as the cornerstone of sustainable business practices and global collaboration. This conference provides an excellent platform for researchers, practitioners, and academicians to exchange ideas, share insights, and inspire new strategies for the future. I congratulate the organizing team for their efforts and extend my best wishes for the success of this event. May the deliberations today ignite pathways for impactful global change.

Warm regards,

Dr. Vasu B A
Principal/Director
Soundarya Institute of Management and Science
Bengaluru Karnataka.

Chief Editor

Dr. Vasu B A is a renowned educator in the field of Commerce and Management, with a strong foundation in both statistics and management. He holds an M.Sc. in Statistics from Bangalore University and a Doctorate in Philosophy (Ph.D.) in Management and Statistics. Dr. Vasu is a life member of the Analytics Society of India (ASI) and has been recognized by IMA Wiley Miles University for his excellence in enabling students to become industry-ready. With over three decades of experience in teaching, research, and consultancy, he has significantly contributed to shaping academic and professional minds. Currently, he serves as the Principal/ Director at Soundarya Institute of Management and Science, Bengaluru, where his leadership and expertise continue to inspire students and faculty alike. His dedication to research, academic growth, and industry relevance has made him a respected figure in the educational community.

Editor

Prof. Vaibhav S Arwade, a highly experienced faculty in the domain of Commerce and Management, holds PG degree in Commerce from prestigious Karnatak University Dharwad and PG Diploma in Business Management from Symbiosis Pune. Being a dynamic educator with over 13 years of teaching expertise coupled with three years of corporate immersion. With a unique international stint, he contributed his skills to Indian companies in West Africa, spanning Ghana, Gambia, Burkina Faso, Benin, and Togo. Beyond the classroom, he's a compassionate soft skills trainer, impacting over 12,000 underprivileged students across India. Recognized for his dedication, he received the "Dr. B R Ambedkar's Youth for Nations Award for Exceptional Service to Underprivileged Students" from J S University Shikohabad, Uttar Pradesh. Prof. Arwade is a fervent researcher, having presented more than 12 research papers in national and international conferences and authored two insightful books. Currently serving as an Assistant Professor in the Department of MBA at Soundarya Institute of Management and Science, Bangalore, he continues to inspire and empower students with his passion for education and social service.

Editor

Mr. Angel Chakraborty, is an accomplished academic professional and subject matter expert (SME), with over 10 years of experience spanning teaching, research, and industry. Currently serving as an Assistant Professor in the MBA department at Soundarya Institute of Management and Science, he specializes in areas like Green Marketing, Operation Management, Supply Chain Management, and Consumer Behavior. He is an engineer turned academician and holds a prestigious MBA Degree in Marketing and Operations from Amity Business School, Amity University, Noida. He has authored 15 research papers, published 1 patent and participated in various global conferences. A proactive mentor and leader, he thrives in fostering innovation and stakeholder engagement.

Editor

Dr. Roopa Shettigar, a dynamic academician and researcher, is an Associate Professor at Soundarya Institute of Management and Science, Bangalore. With a Ph.D. in Management, she has over 20 years of experience in academia and industry. Dr. Shettigar's expertise spans HR, marketing, and organizational effectiveness, with a special focus on employee engagement. She has published numerous papers in reputed journals and conferences, and holds multiple design patents on innovative HR and organizational devices. A recognized leader, Dr. Shettigar has been awarded Best Researcher accolades and serves as an editor and keynote speaker at global forums. Her passion for blending academia with industry practice has made her a trailblazer in her field, empowering future leaders with cutting-edge insights in HR and management.

Editor

G Vasanth Kumar is a dedicated academician and researcher, currently serving as an Assistant Professor. He holds a Master's degree from Christ (Deemed to be University), Bengaluru, and has submitted his Ph.D. thesis in the area of business management. With over five years of academic experience, he specializes in knowledge management, work-life balance, and sustainable business practices. His research contributions include publications in renowned journals such as SCOPUS, Elsevier, and Web of Science. His paper on sustainable employee retention strategies won the Best Research Paper Award at VANICOM 2020, hosted by Pondicherry University. Beyond research, he has actively organized major academic events like "Samshodhan," a national-level research seminar, and "XllenZ 2018," a business fest at Christ University's Lavasa campus. Vasanth Kumar also holds certifications in Google Analytics, Tally ERP 9, and MS Office, bridging theory and industry practice. His passion lies in fostering critical thinking and preparing students for global business challenges.

Editor

Prof. Vibin Krishnan R is currently serving as an Assistant Professor in the Department of Business Administration at Soundarya Institute of Management and Science, Bangalore-73. He holds a Postgraduate degree in Commerce, has cleared K-SET, and is pursuing a Ph.D. in Commerce at Annamalai University.

With two years of corporate experience and five years in academia, he has contributed as a resource person for personality development and training programs. He has presented papers at national and international conferences, with publications in reputed journals.

Committed to innovative teaching methodologies, he has earned a Diploma in Outcome-Based Education, enabling him to design curriculum structures that align with modern educational frameworks. His approach integrates practical learning, student engagement, and research-driven insights, ensuring that education is not just informative but transformative.

INDEX

Sl no	Particulars	Authors	Page no.
1	A Study on Consumer Perception Towards E Shopping With Reference Banglore City"	Amitha H N Sowmya V	21
2	A Study on the Future of Work: HR Innovations and Emerging Remote Work Models	Dr. Champa Ramkrishna Parab	22
3	A Study on the Impact of Modern Marketing Strategies on the Success of New Products	Revathi.M Dr.K.Sarulatha	23
4	Fintech Innovations As a Mediating Mechanism in the Esg–Bank Performance Nexus: Evidence From Indian Banks	Mr. Vaibhav S Arwade Dr. Brammhanada Sharma	24
5	Empirical Analysis of the Influence of AI-Powered Digital Marketing on Consumer Purchase Decisions	Dr. Anthony P. D'Souza Ms. Madhumeeta Dhar	25
6	Digital Payment Systems: Impact on Consumer Spending Behaviour	Tanvi Kurtiker Danica F. Menezes	26
7	Artificial Intelligence and it in Business: A Data-Driven Exploration of Transformation and Growth	Dr. Deepali Gurudas Naik Ms. Madhumeeta Dhar	27
8	Embracing Green: Bridging the Gap Between Sustainable Actions to Sustainable Consumption	Prof Sangeeta Yadav	28
9	Ai-Driven Business Management: Transforming Strategy, Innovation, And Decision-Making	Jeena Raju Ms. Siva Kumari	29
10	SWOC Analysis of the Tourism Industry: Special Reference With the Unesco World Heritage Site of Kaziranga National Park	Bharat Bonia & Prof. Nivedita Goswami	30
11	Crypto Currency Regulations and Their Impact on Investment Trends in India	Ms. Naga Harshitha R.B Prof. Ramya H P	31
12	The Role of Business Analytics in Enhancing Financial Decision-Making	Prof. Yuvaraj Halage Dr. Bharathkumar K K	32
13	Impact of Digital Marketing on Rural Consumer Purchasing Decisions	Dr Manju B Dr. Muthulakshmi P	33
14	Impact of Artificial Intelligence on Mental Accounting Behaviors: Insights From Digital Payment Systems	Khuld Mahfooz Saidalavi K	34
15	AI-Ready Minds- Preparedness of the Rural Students for the AI Driven Job Sector	Mr. Robin Joseph Sera Ms. Vaishnavi Y Acharya Ms. M J Jeena Mary	35

Sl no	Particulars	Authors	Page no.
16	AI-Driven Monitoring and Emotion Recognition for Alzheimer's Patients With Blockchain- Enhanced Data Security	Mr.K.J.S Upendra Chatradi Poojitha Sai Kodirekka Priyanka Marapatla Yeshwanth Machala Siva Krishna Babu Dandu Sri Krisha Babu	36
17	An Impact of Mobile Trading Apps on Investment Decision of Individual Investors	Manjunatha G Manoj Kumar N	37
18	Hybrid Multi-Stage Network for Comprehensive Lung X-Ray Analysis	Mr.S.Sreenivasu T.Sri Lalitha R.A.P.Sowjanya P.Manasa P.Deepika	38
19	Bamboo- Based and Handicrafts in Kalyan Karnataka Region: A New Start-Up Venture	Sharanabasava Hiremath, Dr. Maruthi Rao, Professor	39
20	Environmental Dynamics of Spice Industry in Kerala: A Study based on Cultivation and Export	Nayana. P. A Dr. Roni Jain Raju	40
21	Globalization and Strategic Management: Innovation, Collaboration, and Leadership	Sayyed Sirajuddeen T A	41
22	Indian Healthcare Industry: A Global Perspective	Siddika Banu	42
23	A Study on the Future of Work: HR Innovations and Emerging Remote Work Models	Dr. Champa Ramkrishna Parab	43
24	Identification of Factors and Challenges Affecting Exports of Moradabad Brassware Industry	Ashar Uddin Deepak Bhandari	44
25	An Evaluation of Farmers' Perception on Agricultural Commodity Derivatives	Dr. Shashikumar C R Sunaina K	45
26	Igniting Innovation: A Deep Dive into Entrepreneurship and Startups	Talari Shanthala Neravati Upendra	46
27	The Business of Intellectual Property: A Literature Review of IP Management Research	Roshni Yadav	47
28	Labour in the AI Era: Emergency or Encouragement?	Mahadev Shivagouda Dharigoudar	48
29	A Study on the Impact of Modern Marketing Strategies on the Success of New Products	Revathi. M Dr.K. Sarulatha	49
30	A Study on Student Perception Towards the E-Payment in Bangalore	Maria Anjali L Mr. Manjunatha G	50
31	Impact of Artificial Intelligence on Mental Accounting Behaviors: Insights from Digital Payment Systems	Khuld Mahfooz Saidalavi K	51
32	Analyzing the Effectiveness of Chatbots in Customer Service and Lead Generation	Mr. Manjunatha G Mr. Shivakumar S	52

Sl no	Particulars	Authors	Page no.
33	Role of Biotechnology in Environment based Entrepreneurship	Supriyo Acharya	53
34	The Impact of Artificial Intelligence in Transforming the Accounting Practices	Sridevi Hiremath	54
35	The Impact of Social Media Marketing on Brand Awareness	Sneha D Mr. Manjunatha G	55
36	Virtual Consumerism: Impact of Technology on Buying Behaviour	Dr. Smitha. N. S Ms. Aruna C. S	56
37	A Study on The Future of Work: HR Innovations and Emerging Remote Work Models	Dr. Champa Ramkrishna Parab	57
38	Crypto Currency Regulations and Their Impact on Investment Trends in India	Ms. Naga Harshitha R.B Prof. Ramya H P	58
39	HR Through AI and People Analytics: A Strategic Framework for Workforce Optimization	Md. Tarique Jawaid Dr. Saidalavi K	59
40	Talent Acquisition and Retention in Global Market: A Review on Challenges and the Impact of Latest Innovations in Global Talent Management	Shashikala H	60
41	A Study on the Future of Work: HR Innovations and Emerging Remote Work Models	Dr. Champa Ramkrishna Parab	61
42	Innovation in Logistics Services: A Pestle Analysis of Outsourcing and Governmental Influence	Ms Bandana Yadav Ms. Madhumeeta Dhar	62
43	Artificial Intelligence and it in Business: A Data-Driven Exploration of Transformation and Growth	Dr. Deepali Gurudas Naik Ms. Madhumeeta Dhar	63
44	Embracing Green: Bridging the Gap Between Sustainable Actions to Sustainable Consumption	Prof Sangeeta Yadav	64
45	AI-Driven Business Management: Transforming Strategy, Innovation, and Decision-Making	Ms. Shivakumari Dr. Jeena Raju	65
46	AI-Ready Minds- Preparedness of the Rural Students for the AI Driven Job Sector	Mr. Robin Joseph Sera Ms. Vaishnavi Y Acharya Ms. M J Jeena Mary	66
47	Artificial Intelligence: Machine Learning: Block Chain: Cyber Security: In Procurment 5.0 in Supply Chain	Pallikkara Viswanathan	67
48	A Study on New Innovations in Employee Training and Development	Anupkumar Jamboti	68
49	Impact on the Cryptocurrency and Block Chain Technology on the Financial Sector	Prashanth K Abhishek KD Prof. Shareef AP	69
50	Harnessing User-Generated Content [UGC]: A Strategic Tool for Engagement and Brand Loyalty	Manoj H C Kantharaju R N Mr. Angel Chakraborty	70

Sl no	Particulars	Authors	Page no.
51	A Conceptual Study on Digital Banking and Mobile Payment Platforms	Abhishek N D Rakshith P S Prof. Angel Chakraborty	71
52	Quantum-Enhanced AI: Transforming Machine Learning with Quantum Computing	Sangeetha B R Sandhya S Prof. Angel Chakraborty	72
53	Exploring Customer Perception of Web Analysis and Online Behaviour Tracking in a Survey-Based Approval	Shivaganesh K Sushmitha N Yuvaraj Halage	73
54	The Impact of Social Media Influencers on Consumer Purchasing Behavior: A Comparative Study of Urban and Rural Consumers	Sahana A Lohith K S Yuvaraj Halage	74
55	Assessing Employees Perceptions of Gamification in HR: Ease of Use & Perceived Usefulness	Shwetha B Vinod H. A Yuvaraj Halage	75
56	Exploring the Influence of Corporate Social Responsibility on Brand Image and Consumer Perception	Ms. Chaithra N Mr. Rajesh I N Dr. Roopa Shettigar	76
57	Decoding Employee Mindsets: How AI and NLP Reshape Workplace Culture	Dr. Vasu B.A Monica J Yogashree R	77
58	Decoding Workforce Behaviour: Leveraging Digital Footprints for Predictive HR Analytics	Bhuvana J Shashikala L Angel Chakraborty	78
59	Entrepreneurship in the Gig Era: A New Business Model	Nitheesh B S	79
60	The Adoption of Distributed Ledger Technology in Banking and Finance: Regulatory Challenges and Efficiency Opportunities	Hariprasad Nayak Chandra shekhar G Vasanth kumar	80
61	Assessing the Impact of Human Resource Policies on Women's Career Progression in the Indian Context	Priyanka Y A Sakshi Vaibhav S Arwade	81
62	Impact of Predictive Analytics on Customer Behavior and Engagement in "Balancing Flexibility and Burnout: The Psychological Effects of Remote Work"	Ganika B K Gagana B K G Vasanth Kumar	82
63	Risk Management in Global Markets: Strategies for Financial Stability and Competitive Resilience	Gagana BK Santhosh Angel Chakraborty	83
64	Sustainable Innovations and Market Trends: A Path to Future Growth	Ms. Sushma N Ms. Varsha J Dr. Roopa Shettigar	84

Sl no	Particulars	Authors	Page no.
65	Beyond Conversations: How AI-Powered Chatbots Redefine Customer Experience	Bhavya M T Jeevitha V Prof. Shareef A P	85
66	Exploring Customer Behavior and Profitability: A Survey on How Marketing Analytics Influences Customer and Marketing Behavior in Business Ventures	Akshay kumar G N Madhusudhan D Yuvaraj Halage	86
67	The Role of Business Analytics in Enhancing Financial Decision-Making	Manoj Kumar S Manoj B Yuvaraj Halage	87
68	Sustainability in Business: Strategies for Long-Term Success and Environmental Responsibility	Mr. Mahabaleshwar N Hegde Mr. Karthik G Dr. Roopa Shettigar	88
69	Remote Work and Its Influence on Employee Productivity and Mental Well-Being	Ms. Thanuja A M Ms. Chaithanya T R Dr. Roopa Shettigar	89
70	Leveraging Customer Lifetime Value(LTV) Analytics for Sustainable Growth in Fintech	Ms. Girija M Ms. Vinutha Dr. Roopa Shettigar	90
71	Technological Innovations in Logistics and Transportation: Enhancing Efficiency, Sustainability, and Global Trade	Ganika BK Hemanth Angel Chakraborty	91
72	Retention Revolution: Harnessing Power BI for Attrition Analytics and Sustainable Workforce Success	Vaishnavi V Deepthi S S Prof. Vaibhav S Arwade	92
73	The Dynamic Long Run and Short Run Linkages between Exchange Rates and NSE Nifty 50	Santhosh Yashaswini A Prof. Vaibhav S Arwade	93
74	Bitcoin, Blockchain, and Beyond: The Evolution of Digital Currencies	Aaina Jain Chethan G Dr. Ramesh D	94
75	Advancing Diversity, Equity and Inclusion (DEI) in the Workplace: Strategies, Challenges, and Business Impact	Ms. Thanuja M Ms. Nageshwari k Dr. Roopa Shettigar	95
76	The Evolution and Impact of Digital Marketing in the Modern Business Landscape	Shobhitha R Rakshitha M R Prof. Shareef A P	96
77	The Impact of Artificial Intelligence on HR: AI, Recruitment, Talent Management and Employee Engagement	Mamatha S M Varshini N B Prof. Shareef A P	97

Sl no	Particulars	Authors	Page no.
78	The Impact of ESG Reporting on Performance: Insights from the Indian Banking Sector	Nayana B Nisha K M Prof. Vaibhav S Arwade	98
79	The Role of Private Equity in Indian Aviation	Professor Prema Venkatraman	99
80	Revolutionizing Performance Management: Strategies for Employee Growth and Engagement	Vaishnavi G Teja Babu KP Angel Chakraborty	100
81	AI-Driven Talent Acquisition: Enhancing Recruitment Efficiency and Mitigating Bias in Hiring	Reshmi Raj K V Varshitha H S G Vasanth Kumar	101
82	The Influence of Work-Life Balance on Employee Retention	Yashaswini A Santhosh Prof. Vaibhav S Arwade	102
83	A Study on the Impact of Modern Marketing Strategies on the Success of New Products	Revathi.M Dr.K.Sarulatha	103
84	Digital Payment Systems: Impact on Consumer Spending Behaviour	Tanvi Kurtiker Danica F. Menezes	104
85	Leadership in Remote Work Models: Shaping the Future of Work for a Digital Era	Amruta V Chougule Dr. Sandhya Anvekar	105
	About Department Of MBA		107

A STUDY ON CONSUMER PERCEPTION TOWARDS E SHOPPING WITH REFERENCE BANGLORE CITY

Amitha H N

Assistant Professor
Department of Commerce
Ramaiah Institute of Business Studies
amithanandish@gmail.com

Sowmya V

Assistant Professor
Department of Commerce
Ramaiah Institute of Business Studies
sowmya9025@gmail.com

ABSTRACT

In this paper, our primary objective is to explores the buying perceptions of online buyers in Bengaluru city, focusing on factors such as convenience, product variety, price, product quality and brand reputation. In current market trends most of the people are depending on e shopping in Bengaluru city, as in their busy schedule the online shopping is very convenient platform to purchase anything they want. Some of the people in Bengaluru even today they believe in traditional shopping as they think it is best way to purchase. Businesses can enhance their online shopping experience to attract more customers by offering competitive pricing, a convenient shopping experience, a variety range of products, and building a strong brand. This study provides valuable insights for businesses in Bengaluru, which enabling them to tailor their strategies and meet the evolving need of online customers.

Key words: E-shopping, Traditional shopping, Perception, Brand, Bengaluru.

A STUDY ON THE FUTURE OF WORK: HR INNOVATIONS AND EMERGING REMOTE WORK MODELS

Dr. Champa Ramkrishna Parab

Associate Professor, Department of Commerce
MES Vasant Joshi College of Arts and Commerce, Zuarinagar, Goa
champaparab@gmail.com | 9823162461

ABSTRACT

The future of work is being reshaped by digital transformation, workforce decentralization, and HR innovations that support remote employment. This study explores the evolution of remote work models, focusing on the role of HR in driving workplace innovation and enhancing employee productivity. The research examines emerging digital platforms that facilitate remote employment across industries, assessing their impact on job accessibility, recruitment, and talent management. This study adopts an exploratory research methodology, utilizing qualitative analysis of various remote job boards, freelance marketplaces, and tech-specific employment platforms. Websites such as We Work Remotely, Remote.co, and Flex Jobs provide structured remote job opportunities, while gig platforms like Upwork and Fiverr enable freelancers to connect with global clients. Additionally, tech-focused platforms like Stack Overflow Jobs, GitHub Jobs, and Dice cater to IT and programming professionals seeking remote roles. The research evaluates these platforms based on accessibility, job diversity, security, and user engagement. Key findings reveal that HR innovations, such as AI-driven recruitment, virtual collaboration tools, and digital performance tracking, have become essential for managing remote teams. The study also highlights challenges such as work-life balance, job security, and employer expectations in remote settings. These insights contribute to understanding how HR strategies can foster a more inclusive and sustainable remote work environment.The implications of this research are significant for businesses, HR professionals, and job seekers navigating the evolving job market. By leveraging digital platforms and HR technology, organizations can enhance remote workforce efficiency, attract top talent, and remain competitive in the future of work.

Keywords: Remote Work, HR Innovation, Future, Digital Platforms, Freelancing, Workforce, Recruitment.

A STUDY ON THE IMPACT OF MODERN MARKETING STRATEGIES ON THE SUCCESS OF NEW PRODUCTS

Revathi.M

PhD Research Scholar (Part-Time)
Rvs College Of Arts and Science
Sulur, Coimbatore.

Dr.K.Sarulatha

Assistant Professor
School of Business Management
RVS College of Arts and Science
Sulur, Coimbatore

ABSTRACT

Modern marketing methods have changed to take use of innovative technologies and innovative strategies in the current digital world. These tactics cover a broad spectrum, such as influencer collaborations, content marketing, social media interaction, data-driven marketing, and search engine optimization (SEO). Businesses may better target certain consumers with their marketing campaigns by utilizing big data and analytics. The environment has also changed as a result of the growth of mobile marketing and customized customer experiences, which enables businesses to communicate with customers instantly. All things considered, contemporary marketing tactics emphasize developing deep, tailored connections that increase engagement and cultivate brand loyalty. The purpose of this study is to examine at the significance modern methods of marketing are to a new product's success. The potential impact of contemporary marketing techniques, such as influencer, content, loyalty, social media, and targeted email campaigns, on increasing the success rate of new goods is evaluated. The goal of the study is to show how a new product's overall performance is correlated with the use of various contemporary marketing strategies.

Keywords: Modern Marketing Strategies, Digital Marketing Techniques , Influencer and Social Media Marketing, Customer Engagement and Brand Loyalty, Data-Driven and Targeted Marketing.

FINTECH INNOVATIONS AS A MEDIATING MECHANISM IN THE ESG–BANK PERFORMANCE NEXUS: EVIDENCE FROM INDIAN BANKS

Mr. Vaibhav S Arwade

Dr. Brammhanada Sharma

ABSTRACT

In an era of growing emphasis on sustainable finance, Environmental, Social, and Governance (ESG) practices have emerged as acute pillars of responsible banking. Simultaneously, Fintech innovations are redesigning the financial services landscape by improving efficiency, transparency, and inclusivity. This study examines the mediating role of Fintech innovations in the relationship between ESG practices and bank performance, using evidence from Indian banks. Drawing upon the resource-based view and stakeholder theory, the research examines how digital transformation through Fintech enhances the effectiveness of ESG initiatives in delivering improved performance outcomes. A structured survey was conducted with 150 professionals across five leading Indian banks—spanning both public and private sectors—based in Bengaluru North. The study employed **Structural Equation Modeling (SEM)** via **AMOS** to analyze causal relationships, and **Confirmatory Factor Analysis (CFA)** to validate construct reliability and model fit. **Baron and Kenny's mediation approach**, supported by **bootstrapping techniques**, was applied to assess the mediating impact of Fintech innovations. The results confirm that ESG dimensions have a significant positive impact on bank performance, and this relationship is notably strengthened through Fintech applications such as AI-based credit risk models, block chain-enabled compliance, and digital customer engagement tools. Fintech acts as a dynamic enabler, bridging sustainability goals with operational efficiency and financial performance. The study offers valuable insights for banking leaders and policymakers aiming to integrate ESG frameworks with Fintech strategies. It contributes to the growing body of literature on sustainable digital banking and underscores the strategic importance of Fintech in achieving ESG-aligned performance in the Indian banking context.

Keywords: Fintech Innovations, ESG Practices, Bank Performance, Sustainable Finance, Mediation Analysis.

EMPIRICAL ANALYSIS OF THE INFLUENCE OF AI-POWERED DIGITAL MARKETING ON CONSUMER PURCHASE DECISIONS

Dr. Anthony P. D'Souza

Associate Professor,
Commerce Department,
Fr. Agnel College of Arts and Commerce, Pilar Goa

Ms. Madhumeeta Dhar

Assistant Professor,
GVM College of commerce and Economics Ponda Goa

ABSTRACT

Artificial Intelligence (AI) has transformed the marketing arena by allowing businesses to provide very personalized experiences to consumers. By using machine learning algorithms, predictive analytics, and data-driven insights, AI has enabled marketers to personalize their approaches, connect better with consumers, and maximize their marketing efforts. In digital marketing, AI-based personalization is being utilized to a greater extent to forecast consumer preferences, produce customized content, and improve customer experiences overall. As digital marketing is constantly changing, the use of AI in driving consumer behavior has gained even greater visibility, especially in deciding what to buy. This study analyzes the influence of AI-driven digital marketing on Goan consumer buying decisions, focusing on how AI-driven personalization shapes the behavior of consumers online. The primary objective of this study is to analyze the impact of AI-driven marketing strategies on consumer purchasing intentions, focusing on statistical test outcomes. 200 participants were selected from Goa, with information being collected from those in the marketing field and those on online platforms. The random sampling method was employed, and the collected data was analyzed using Explanatory Factor Analysis (EFA). Demographic analysis revealed that the respondents were representative in terms of age groups and types of businesses. The results were interpreted on the basis of KMO and Bartlett's Test, Rotated Component Matrix, and Reliability Statistics to make substantial inferences. This study provides useful information about the impact of AI technology in personalized marketing efforts and its collective influence on the consumer decision-making processes across industries.

Keywords: AI-Powered Digital Marketing, Consumer Purchase Decisions, Personalization, Explanatory Factor Analysis, Consumer Behavior.

DIGITAL PAYMENT SYSTEMS: IMPACT ON CONSUMER SPENDING BEHAVIOUR

Tanvi Kurtiker

Assistant Professor,
Department of Economics,
Dnyanprassarak Mandal's College and Research Centre, Assagao-Goa.
Tanvi@dmscollege.ac.in

Danica F. Menezes

Assistant Professor
Department of Economics
Dnyanprassarak Mandal's College and Research Centre, Assagao-Goa.
Danica@dmscollege.ac.in

ABSTRACT

Increased adoption of digital payment systems in current times has transformed consumer spending behavior significantly changing the traditional purchasing patterns. The present study tries to explore the impact of digital payment methods among the young crowd. The paper tries to examine the psychological and economic implications of cashless transactions, analyzing consumption and the possible challenges associated with the same. Additionally, it investigates demographic and social differences in adoption of digital payment methods. Methodology to be adopted for the study is non probability sampling technique and the data collection tool for the same is structured questionnaire and interview.

Key Words : Digital Payments, Cashless Transactions, Psychological and Economic Implications.

ARTIFICIAL INTELLIGENCE AND IT IN BUSINESS: A DATA-DRIVEN EXPLORATION OF TRANSFORMATION AND GROWTH

Dr. Deepali Gurudas Naik

Assistant professor, Department of commerce. Goa vidyaprasarak mandal's Gopal govind poy raiturcar college of commerce and economics Farmagudi ponda goa.
naikdeepali17@gmail.com , 9637214287

Ms. Madhumeeta Dhar

Assistant Professor, GVM College of Commerce and Economics Ponda Goa
Madhumeetadhar2029@gmail.com

ABSTRACT

The exponential growth in Information Technology (IT) and Artificial Intelligence (AI) has revolutionized business activities, market frameworks, and economic performance globally. This research delves into the extensive impact of IT and AI on business through the use of secondary data obtained from Internet World Stats, Digital Market Outlook and other academic sources. A thorough review of literature and documentary research approach were used in gathering relevant information, emphasizing main variables like internet penetration, digitalization, and ICT integration into business. Descriptive analysis, the research study analyzes trends in international internet usage and digitization of businesses, while statistical methods like correlation and regression are used to analyze the impact of IT adoption on business performance measures. The findings indicate the implications of AI-based decision-making, automation, and connectivity in making businesses more efficient, scalable, and competitive. The research study also examines issues like risks of cyber security threats, digital divide, and ethics related to AI adoption in business. Through the integration of empirical evidence and scholarly literature, this study offers a critical appreciation of how IT and AI are reshaping business environments, driving economic development, and determining future technological directions. The study's implications are far-reaching to policymakers, business executives, and researchers, providing a basis for strategic decision-making in the changing digital economy.

Keywords: IT adoption, Artificial Intelligence, Digital transformation, Business performance, Growth.

EMBRACING GREEN: BRIDGING THE GAP BETWEEN SUSTAINABLE ACTIONS TO SUSTAINABLE CONSUMPTION

Prof Sangeeta Yadav,

School of Management & Commerce, Garden City University

ABSTRACT

As environment- and health-conscious consumers increasingly shift their preferences towards organic and eco-friendly lifestyles, businesses are leveraging this trend by adopting Green Production (GP) and Green Marketing (GM) strategies. Firms such as Pro Nature, 24 Mantra Organic, Down To Earth, Organic Tattva, and global brands like Zara (Inditex) have embraced sustainable practices to cater to this growing demand. This empirical study examines Green Consumption Behavioural (GCB) Trends among consumers in the metropolitan cities of Bangalore and Hyderabad, analysing their purchasing preferences and sustainability-driven choices. By identifying key drivers and barriers to Sustainable Consumption, the study offers insights into how green interventions can shape consumer behaviour and corporate sustainability strategies. The findings contribute to the broader discourse on environmental responsibility and offer actionable recommendations for businesses and policymakers aiming to foster a greener economy.

Key words: Green Marketing, Green interventions, Sustainable Consumption.

AI-DRIVEN BUSINESS MANAGEMENT: TRANSFORMING STRATEGY, INNOVATION, AND DECISION-MAKING

Jeena Raju

HOD MBA Department, Patel Institute of Science and Management,
Bangalore pismjeena@gmail.com

Ms. Siva Kumari

MBA Student
Patel Institute of science & Management

ABSTRACT

Artificial Intelligence (AI) and Machine Learning (ML) are revolutionizing business management by enhancing strategic decision-making, improving efficiency, and fostering innovation. This conceptual study explores the transformative role of AI-driven technologies in key business functions, including strategy development, marketing, supply chain management, and customer engagement. AI enables organizations to harness large datasets, apply predictive analytics, and automate processes, leading to data-driven insights and improved operational agility. The study examines how AI contributes to competitive advantage by optimizing resource allocation, reducing operational costs, and enhancing customer experiences through personalized recommendations and intelligent automation. Additionally, AI-driven business management enhances risk assessment and fraud detection, ensuring more secure and transparent operations. However, integrating AI into business processes presents challenges such as data privacy concerns, ethical implications, and workforce displacement. Addressing these challenges requires a balanced approach that combines technological advancements with human oversight and ethical AI frameworks. Furthermore, the study highlights the need for businesses to invest in AI literacy and workforce upskilling to maximize AI's potential while ensuring job roles evolve alongside technological advancements. The findings suggest that AI-driven management approaches lead to greater efficiency, innovation, and adaptability in a rapidly changing business environment. As AI continues to evolve, future research should focus on its long-term impact on leadership, decision-making and sustainable business strategies. This study provides a conceptual foundation for understanding AI's role in modern business management, emphasizing both opportunities and challenges in leveraging AI for strategic and operational success.

Keywords: Artificial Intelligence, Machine Learning, Business Management, Predictive Analytics, Automation, Innovation.

SWOC ANALYSIS OF THE TOURISM INDUSTRY: SPECIAL REFERENCE WITH THE UNESCO WORLD HERITAGE SITE OF KAZIRANGA NATIONAL PARK

Bharat Bonia & Prof. Nivedita Goswami

ABSTRACT

The tourism industry has an immense impact on the economy and the local community. From new employment generation to poverty reduction, and cultural development to bring peace among the communities, tourism has a unique impact. The tourism industry plays an active role in the economic, environmental, and socio-cultural aspects, of the study area or locality, and has both positive and negative impacts. To minimize the negative consequences both on the environment and on the local community, it is important to analyze the strengths, weaknesses, opportunities, and challenges in the study area so that further tourism development takes place and the environment must be protected and preserved sustainably. The tourism industry is facing several challenges, and the development efforts of this industry are not sustainable. This study uses the SWOC/ SWOT (strengths, weaknesses, opportunities, and challenges/Threats) model to chart out a path for the tourism business in Kaziranga National Park to grow sustainably. Kaziranga National Park was designated a UNESCO World Heritage site in recognition of its distinctive natural environment and habitat for 70% of the world's one-horned rhinoceroses. It is one of seven such heritage sites in India. The information utilized in this study came from a variety of sources, including a review of the literature and interviews with people who worked directly for tourism-related firms or enterprises in the studied area. The results of this work revealed that the tourism industry in the Kaziranga National Park has various opportunities for further development as wildlife tourism and ecotourism hub of India and the world at large.

Keywords: Strengths; Weaknesses, Opportunities; Challenges; Sustainable; Environment; Kaziranga.

CRYPTO CURRENCY REGULATIONS AND THEIR IMPACT ON INVESTMENT TRENDS IN INDIA

Ms. Naga Harshitha R.B

Student

Department of Management Studies, Dayananda Sagar College of Engineering

harshithabadri0@gmail.com

ORCID ID: https://orcid.org/**0009-0002-4012-967X**

Prof. Ramya H P

Assistant Professor

Department of Management Studies, Dayananda Sagar College of Engineering

ramya-mbavtu@dayanadasagar.edu

ORCID ID: https://orcid.org/0000-0002-2048-807X

ABSTRACT

Cryptocurrency is one of the most popular investment products in India that attracted retail as well as institutional investors, but the regulatory framework surrounding cryptocurrency markets remains uncertain, which creates challenges for various stakeholders. A good understanding of impacts has to be made for policy-making that encourages innovation while ensuring market stability. Since global research extensively covers the regulation of cryptocurrency, the specific policies for India remain unclear and silent about how these will be shaping investment trends. This study aims to bridge that gap by tracing the evolution of cryptocurrency regulations and how the latter will influence investor trust, trading patterns, and the overall dynamics in Indian markets through an analysis of government reports, market research, articles, and trends in cryptocurrencies.

The findings depict how regulations impact investor trust and sometimes lead to a change in trading volumes and patterns. How investors preferred other platforms at times of strict policies and how transparent and stable regulations have helped more participation. It also shows the need for an equilibrist regulatory framework, which will enhance innovation but keep investors protected. This insight will offer actionable recommendations for stakeholders to adapt to the changing cryptocurrency landscape in India.

Keywords: Cryptocurrency regulations, Investment trends, Regulatory framework, Market dynamics.

THE ROLE OF BUSINESS ANALYTICS IN ENHANCING FINANCIAL DECISION-MAKING

Prof. Yuvaraj Halage

Assistant Professor
Department of MBA
Soundarya Institute of Management and Science
Email: wisdom.yuvaraj@gmail.com

Dr. Bharathkumar K K

Associate Professor
Department of Management Sciences
Maharaja Institute of Technology
Email: bharath.kariappa@gmail.com

ABSTRACT

The integration of predictive analytics in banking has revolutionized the way institutions interact with customers, offering personalized services and enhancing decision-making processes. This study investigates the influence of predictive analytics on customer behavior and engagement in global banking, with a focus on understanding how data-driven innovations affect customer satisfaction, trust, and loyalty. A survey-based approach is utilized, targeting bank customers across various regions to assess their perceptions of predictive tools such as personalized offers, fraud detection, and loan recommendations. The findings suggest that predictive analytics positively impacts customer engagement by delivering tailored banking experiences, improving trust through proactive services, and fostering long-term loyalty. However, regional differences in customer responses to these technologies are observed, highlighting varying levels of trust and acceptance based on cultural and economic factors. This paper contributes to the growing body of literature on digital transformation in banking by shedding light on the ways predictive analytics reshape customer behavior, offering insights into how global banking institutions can leverage these tools to optimize service delivery and enhance customer relationships. The study also presents practical implications for banks seeking to implement predictive analytics strategies, with an emphasis on creating customer-centric solutions that drive both satisfaction and business growth.

Keywords: Predictive Analytics, Customer Behavior, Customer Engagement, Trust, Global Banking, Digital Transformation

IMPACT OF DIGITAL MARKETING ON RURAL CONSUMER PURCHASING DECISIONS

Dr Manju B

Assistant Professor, Department of Commerce and Management,
CHRIST (Deemed to be University), Chandapura, Bangalore
muthulakshmi.p@christuniversity.in

Dr. Muthulakshmi P

Assistant Professor, School of Business and Management – BBA,
Swamy Vivekananda Rural First Grade College, Bangalore
manjumahesha.mk@gmail.com

ABSTRACT

Consumer purchasing decisions are deeply influenced by their behavior, which has evolved significantly under the impact of digital marketing. With the rapid adoption of mobile phones, these devices have become indispensable, serving as a vital medium through which digital marketing influences consumer choices. This study aims to explore the effects of digital marketing on rural consumers' purchasing decisions, focusing on the growing digital penetration that has brought rural areas on par with urban regions. The research examines four essential aspects of digital marketing: mobile marketing, content marketing, social media marketing, and email marketing, each playing a distinct role in shaping purchase behavior. The study is grounded in four hypotheses designed to analyze the individual and combined impact of these parameters on rural consumer behavior. Data collected from rural regions highlights the transformative role of digital marketing in enhancing accessibility to information, altering traditional buying patterns, and fostering a more informed consumer base. The study's findings are expected to contribute to a deeper understanding of how businesses can leverage digital marketing strategies to effectively target rural consumers, ensuring inclusivity and driving growth in these untapped markets.

Key words: Consumer behaviour, Mobile marketing, Content marketing, Rural consumers, Email marketing, Social media marketing.

IMPACT OF ARTIFICIAL INTELLIGENCE ON MENTAL ACCOUNTING BEHAVIORS: INSIGHTS FROM DIGITAL PAYMENT SYSTEMS

Khuld Mahfooz

Research Scholar, Department of Management and Commerce,
Maulana Azad National Urdu University, Hyderabad

Saidalavi K

Assistant Professor, Department of Management and Commerce,
Maulana Azad National Urdu University, Hyderabad

Abstract

This study provides a comprehensive review of the role of artificial intelligence (AI) in influencing mental accounting behaviors within the context of digital payment systems. Mental accounting, a cognitive process wherein individuals categorize and perceive money differently based on its source or intended use, often diverges from the principle of fungibility. The research investigates how AI-driven technologies impact consumers' budgeting, spending, saving, and investment behaviors, with a particular focus on the cognitive and behavioral nuances of mental accounting. Through an extensive review of existing literature, this study highlights the dual-edged effects of AI on financial decision-making, including the potential for improved financial management alongside challenges such as expense misclassification, diminished awareness of spending patterns, and an overreliance on algorithmic insights that may misalign with personal financial objectives. The findings offer significant practical implications, providing a nuanced understanding of the interplay between AI technologies and consumer financial behavior. This study contributes to the field by offering actionable recommendations for the design of AI systems that support more informed, autonomous, and responsible financial decision-making, thereby addressing critical gaps in the understanding of AI's role in consumer finance.

Keywords: Artificial Intelligence, Mental Accounting, Digital Payment Systems.

AI-READY MINDS- PREPAREDNESS OF THE RURAL STUDENTS FOR THE AI DRIVEN JOB SECTOR

Mr. Robin Joseph Sera

Lecturer in Commerce, Sacred Heart College, Madanthyar,
robinsera361@gmail.com, 9964996649

Ms. Vaishnavi Y Acharya

M.com Previous, Sacred Heart College Madanthyar,
vaishnavi.y.acharyaa@gmail.com, 8050357688,

Ms. M J Jeena Mary

M.com Previous, Sacred Heart College Madanthyar, ,
jeenamarymj@gmail.com, 8904280985

ABSTRACT

There was a paradigm shift in the thought process of people when human labour was replaced by machines during the industrial revolution. It opened new opportunities and insights. This leads the industries to scale up the operation that is ever imagined. The labour force found the new competitor, which is more efficient and cost effective. The AI revolution forced the people to adapt the new skills and traits to escape from the 'pink slip'. The Graduates and other job seekers who hails from rural colleges are waiting to dwell into the job market are conscious about Artificial intelligence and rigorously trying to upgrade their digital skills. The Higher education and system and institutional are also not left behind in this race. The introduction of National education policy 2020 and Introduction of AI related courses in the traditional programs syllabi is a perfect exemplify the commitment to instill the AI skillset among the students. The study focuses on students at Mangalore University with aim: To assess the current state of AI Related education in the curriculum, to evaluate the effectiveness of AI skill development programs in education, to understand the perception of rural students towards AI driven Job Sector and to find the methods to incorporate in curriculum to instill the AI skills. The research involves the quantitative approaches considering the data from primary and secondary sources. The findings of the research are expected to bridge the gap between academic preparation and dynamic requirements for AI driven job sector

Keywords: AI-driven Job sector, digital skills, Artificial intelligent education National education policy 2020, skill development.

AI-DRIVEN MONITORING AND EMOTION RECOGNITION FOR ALZHEIMER'S PATIENTS WITH BLOCKCHAIN- ENHANCED DATA SECURITY

Mr.K.J.S Upendra

Dept. of Artificial Intelligence
Vishnu Institute Of Technology
Andhra Pradesh,India

Chatradi Poojitha Sai

Dept. of Artificial Intelligence
Vishnu Institute Of Technology
Andhra Pradesh,India
21pa1a5422@vishnu.edu.in

Kodirekka Priyanka

Dept. of Artificial Intelligence
Vishnu Institute Of Technology
Andhra Pradesh,India
21pa1a5446@vishnu.edu.in

Marapatla Yeshwanth

Dept. of Artificial Intelligence
Vishnu Institute Of Technology
Andhra Pradesh,India
21pa1a5462@vishnu.edu.in

Machala Siva Krishna Babu

Dept. of Artificial Intelligence
Vishnu Institute Of Technology
Andhra Pradesh,India
21pa1a5459@vishnu.edu.in

Dandu Sri Krisha Babu

Dept. of Artificial Intelligence
Vishnu Institute Of Technology
Andhra Pradesh,India
22pa5a5403@vishnu.edu.in

ABSTRACT

This paper presents the development of an integrated system for real-time emotion and motion detection aimed at enhancing the care and monitoring of individuals with Alzheimer's disease. Alzheimer's, which affects millions worldwide, leads to severe cognitive decline, making it difficult for patients to express emotions or communicate their needs. The proposed system combines artificial intelligence (AI) and machine learning (ML) to detect both motion-related events (such as falls, unconsciousness, or dizziness) and emotional states (such as happiness, sadness, and anger). Using YOLO (You Only Look Once) for motion detection and a deep learning-based model for facial emotion analysis, the system processes video data through OpenCV for real-time analysis. The backend, powered by Flask, supports event logging and visualization through an interactive web interface, while SQLite stores event logs for ongoing analysis. Additionally, the integration of blockchain technology ensures the security and privacy of sensitive patient data, providing a tamper-proof framework for storing and accessing patient records. The system also triggers audio alerts for critical motion incidents, ensuring quick responses to emergencies. This lightweight yet comprehensive solution provides caregivers and healthcare providers with valuable insights into the emotional and physical well-being of patients, improving their quality of life and offering a new approach to managing Alzheimer's care

Keywords: AI-Based Monitoring, Motion Detection, Emotion Detection, Flask, SQLite, Object Detection, YOLOv8, OpenCV, TensorFlow, Real-Time Surveillance.

AN IMPACT OF MOBILE TRADING APPS ON INVESTMENT DECISION OF INDIVIDUAL INVESTORS

Manjunatha G

Assistant Professor, PG Department of Commerce,
St Claret College Autonomous Bengaluru-560013
E mail- gmanjunatha@claretcollege.edu.in

Manoj Kumar N

Student M com, PG department of Commerce
St Claret College Autonomous, Bengaluru-5600013
Email- n.manumanojkumar@gmail.com

ABSTRACT

Investors have been using mobile trading apps more and more in recent years to purchase stocks, bonds, and mutual funds. The purpose of this study was to investigate how mobile trading apps affect the choices made by individual investors. App suggestions, ratings, usability, personalization, and perceived information are among the important variables examined. Data from 200 respondents was gathered for the study using a purposive sampling technique, and it was then examined using regression, correlation, chi-square, and percentage analysis. The findings show that investor decisions are greatly influenced by mobile trading apps. These results can aid businesses in creating trading apps that suit investor preferences and help potential investors make well-informed decisions.

Keywords: Mobile Trading Apps, Investor Decision-Making , Usability and Personalization in Trading , Financial Technology (FinTech) Adoption, Impact of Trading Apps on Investments.

HYBRID MULTI-STAGE NETWORK FOR COMPREHENSIVE LUNG X-RAY ANALYSIS

Mr.S.Sreenivasu

Guide, Department of Information technology,Shri Vishnu Engineering College for women
Bhimavaram, India. sreenivasu@svecw.edu.in

T.Sri Lalitha

Department of Information technology,Shri Vishnu Engineering College for women
Bhimavaram, India. 21b01a12i0@svecw.edu.in

R.A.P.Sowjanya

Department of Information technology,Shri Vishnu Engineering College for women
Bhimavaram, India. 21b01a12f5@svecw.edu.in

P.Manasa

Department of Information technology,Shri Vishnu Engineering College for women
Bhimavaram, India. 21b01a12d4@svecw.edu.in

P.Deepika

Department of Information technology,Shri Vishnu Engineering College for women
Bhimavaram, India. 21b01a12e9@svecw.edu.in

ABSTRACT

Rapid and accurate diagnosis of repository diseases like COVID-19 and viral pneumonia using chest X-rays (CXRs) is vital. Traditional diagnostic methods often face challenges due to variability in image quality and subtle disease manifestations. This study introduces a hybrid multi-stage network for lung segmentation, disease classification, and severity localization from CXR images. Using the COVID-19 Radiography Database, which includes 3616 COVID-19, 10,192 normal, and 1345 viral pneumonia images, the network employs a U-Net for lung segmentation, followed by disease classification using ResNet and localization with Grad-CAM. Experiments results highlight the network's robust performance across multiple architectures, demonstrating high accuracy in segmentation and classification tasks. The proposed method enhances diagnostic precision and offers clear visual insights into disease severity supporting effective and timely medical intervention.

Keywords: Computer-Aided diagnosis (CAD), Chest X-Ray Analysis, Respiratory Disease Diagnosis, Lung Segmentation, Disease Classification, Severity localization, Deep Learning, Medical Image Analysis.

BAMBOO- BASED AND HANDICRAFTS IN KALYAN KARNATAKA REGION: A NEW START-UP VENTURE

Sharanabasava Hiremath,

Research Scholar,
Dept. of MBA, Rani Channamma University, Belagavi.
sharan.9296@gmail.com, 9986010255

Dr. Maruthi Rao, Professor

Dept. of MBA, Rani Channamma University, Belagavi.

ABSTRACT

This study explores the traditional bamboo and pottery handicrafts in Kalyana Karnataka, shedding light on their historical significance, current challenges, and future potential. These crafts are vital for rural economies, providing jobs for many artisans. However, the sector faces hurdles such as a lack of modernization, insufficient financial support, and weak market connections. In this paper, we look into the obstacles artisans encounter, assess government initiatives, and propose strategies to sustain and grow these crafts. The findings highlight the necessity for government backing, skill development, branding, and digital marketing to help this sector flourish. We conclude with recommendations aimed at enhancing artisans livelihoods and increasing the visibility of bamboo and pottery crafts in global markets.

Keywords: Bamboo handicrafts, Pottery, Kalyana Karnataka, Traditional crafts, Artisan development, Market trends, Government initiatives.

ENVIRONMENTAL DYNAMICS OF SPICE INDUSTRY IN KERALA: A STUDY BASED ON CULTIVATION AND EXPORT

Nayana. P. A

Research Scholar
Research and Post Graduate Department of Commerce
St. Thomas College, Ranni

Dr. Roni Jain Raju

Research Guide and Assistant Professor
Research and Post Graduate Department of Commerce
St. Thomas College, Ranni

ABSTRACT

Kerala is well known for wide variety of spices from ancient time onwards. The spice industry is one of the important contributors to the economy of the state. This research study examines the environmental dynamics of spice industry in Kerala, focusing on its cultivation and export. The study aims to assess the environmental impact on spice industry of Kerala in economic terms. It also analyzes the effect of spice cultivation on the environment and its impact on the livelihood of the stakeholders. The study identifies strategies for sustainable spice cultivation and export. A mixed- method approach will be used for collecting quantitative and qualitative data. Primary data will be collected from spice cultivators, exporters and other related stakeholders. Secondary data will be obtained from government reports and research studies. The study's key findings indicate that spice industry in Kerala has a significant implication on environment such as deforestation, soil degradation, pollution and man animal conflict. The study also reveals that the environmental factors such as climate change, change in precipitation pattern have a severe impact on production, productivity and export of spice in Kerala. However, the study identifies sustainable and climate resilient spice cultivation practices to overcome these problems. The implications of this study highlight the need for sustainable and climate resilient practices in spice industry of Kerala. The study will contribute towards making an environment friendly spice industry in Kerala.

Keywords: environment, spice industry, sustainable, climate - resilient.

GLOBALIZATION AND STRATEGIC MANAGEMENT: INNOVATION, COLLABORATION, AND LEADERSHIP

Sayyed Sirajuddeen T A

B.com (Bangalore North University)

ABSTRACT

In an era of rapid globalization, cross-border collaborations and strategic partnerships have emerged as critical tools for sustainable economic growth and community development. This study explores the role of multinational alliances, innovations in international trade and logistics, and transformative leadership in a post-pandemic world. The study employs a mixed-methods approach, integrating qualitative case studies of successful global partnerships with quantitative data on trade and logistics advancements. Key findings indicate that businesses leveraging technology-driven supply chains, digital trade platforms, and agile leadership strategies have demonstrated resilience and adaptability in the face of economic disruptions. For instance, the World Trade Organization's (WTO) 2023 report highlights how digital trade agreements and AI-driven logistics have accelerated supply chain efficiency, benefiting developing economies. Additionally, collaborations between multinational corporations and local enterprises, such as Starbucks' ethical sourcing initiative and Tesla's joint ventures in Asia, have created job opportunities, facilitated knowledge transfer, fostering economic empowerment at the grassroots level. The implications of these findings emphasize the need for innovative business models that integrate global leadership strategies with community-centric approaches. This paper suggests that future global business strategies should embrace digital transformation, sustainable trade practices, and ethical leadership. By aligning corporate goals with community well-being, businesses can enhance their market position while contributing to social and economic progress in the post-pandemic landscape.

Keywords: Globalization, Strategic Management, Cross-Border Collaboration, International Trade, Digital Transformation, Post-Pandemic Leadership to uplift communities.

INDIAN HEALTHCARE INDUSTRY: A GLOBAL PERSPECTIVE

Siddika Banu

Ph.D. Scholar, Department of Economics, Tripura University,
siddibanu43@gmail.com

ABSTRACT

A study of healthcare is trivial for getting overall insights into the extent of human development of any country. In India, the healthcare sector is one of the largest growing sectors in the economy. It is a highly recognized sector both in terms of revenue generation and employment creation. With the growing demand for healthcare services and products, the healthcare industry has been experiencing a drastic change both in terms of demand and supply side in recent times. The increased growth of the healthcare industry is a consequence of higher economic growth, rising middle-class incomes, and increased healthcare marketing of health insurance providers. The current healthcare system in India comprises a set of public and private institutions, controlled by the state government, the central government, and private organizations. This study focuses on the current status of the Indian healthcare industry and its challenges. Moreover, a comparison would be made between India and some developed and developing countries to have some vivid insights into the health sector. The reports published by WHO and the government of India's reports on health statistics have been used in this study. It is evident that the U.S.A, Canada, China, and Brazil have performed better than India in terms of achievement in healthcare indicators but when compared to other developing countries like Pakistan and Bangladesh, the attainment is better in India.

Keywords: Healthcare industry, India, challenges, developed and developing countries.

A STUDY ON THE FUTURE OF WORK: HR INNOVATIONS AND EMERGING REMOTE WORK MODELS

Dr. Champa Ramkrishna Parab

Associate Professor, Department of Commerce
MES Vasant Joshi College of Arts and Commerce, Zuarinagar, Goa
champaparab@gmail.com | 9823162461

ABSTRACT

The future of work is being reshaped by digital transformation, workforce decentralization, and HR innovations that support remote employment. This study explores the evolution of remote work models, focusing on the role of HR in driving workplace innovation and enhancing employee productivity. The research examines emerging digital platforms that facilitate remote employment across industries, assessing their impact on job accessibility, recruitment, and talent management. This study adopts an exploratory research methodology, utilizing qualitative analysis of various remote job boards, freelance marketplaces, and tech-specific employment platforms. Websites such as We Work Remotely, Remote.co, and FlexJobs provide structured remote job opportunities, while gig platforms like Upwork and Fiverr enable freelancers to connect with global clients. Additionally, tech-focused platforms like Stack Overflow Jobs, GitHub Jobs, and Dice cater to IT and programming professionals seeking remote roles. The research evaluates these platforms based on accessibility, job diversity, security, and user engagement. Key findings reveal that HR innovations, such as AI-driven recruitment, virtual collaboration tools, and digital performance tracking, have become essential for managing remote teams. The study also highlights challenges such as work-life balance, job security, and employer expectations in remote settings. These insights contribute to understanding how HR strategies can foster a more inclusive and sustainable remote work environment. The implications of this research are significant for businesses, HR professionals, and job seekers navigating the evolving job market. By leveraging digital platforms and HR technology, organizations can enhance remote workforce efficiency, attract top talent, and remain competitive in the future of work.

Keywords: Remote Work, HR Innovation, Future, Digital Platforms, Freelancing, Workforce, Recruitment.

IDENTIFICATION OF FACTORS AND CHALLENGES AFFECTING EXPORTS OF MORADABAD BRASSWARE INDUSTRY

Ashar Uddin

Faculty of Commerce and Management, Maulana Azad University, Jodhpur, Rajasthan
asharuddin2016@gmail.com

Deepak Bhandari

Faculty of Commerce and Management, Maulana Azad University, Jodhpur, Rajasthan
deepak_bhandari75@yahoo.com

ABSTRACT

The Moradabad Brassware Industry, renowned for its exquisite craftsmanship, faces significant challenges in maximizing its export potential. This paper explores the various factors and challenges hindering the Moradabad Brassware industry's growth in the global market. (Banerjee, S., 2017) The research identifies limitations in production processes, inadequate design and marketing strategies, fluctuating raw material prices, complex regulatory environments, and labour issues as key factors affecting exports. Additionally, the paper discusses the challenges faced by exporters, including competition from cheaper alternatives, meeting international quality standards, and navigating intricate trade policies. (Sharma, A.K., 2006) Finally, the paper proposes recommendations to overcome these challenges, including industry modernization, design innovation, improved marketing and branding, and policy advocacy for streamlined export procedures. Addressing these factors and challenges is crucial for the Moradabad Brassware Industry to thrive in the international marketplace and preserve its rich heritage for generations to come. (Fink, A., 2005).

Keywords: Material Price, Complex Regulatory, Design Innovation, Streamlined Export, Marketing Strategies.

AN EVALUATION OF FARMERS' PERCEPTION ON AGRICULTURAL COMMODITY DERIVATIVES

Dr. Shashikumar C R

Associate Professor, Department of Commerce,
RNS First Grade College, Bangalore.

Sunaina K

Department of MBA,
RNS First Grade College, Bangalore.

ABSTRACT

Commodity derivative markets in India has a long history. The operations in this segment have however been topsy-turvy. Frequent bans on trading had somewhat retarded the growth of derivatives market in India. The adoption of liberalised economic policies saw the change in the attitude of policy makers and this led to the establishment of exchanges which offered online trading on multi-commodities. However, the stakeholder group which ought to be benefited the most, at least in papers were often neglected. The present study is intended to find out the perception of farmers regarding the functioning of commodity futures markets in India. The study brings to light the source of information regarding derivative trading, their involvement in trading, the problems faced by farmers which keep them away from frequent trading and their opinion on overall impact of agricultural commodity futures.

Key Terms: Derivatives, Futures, Hedging, Commodity Exchanges.

IGNITING INNOVATION: A DEEP DIVE INTO ENTREPRENEURSHIP AND STARTUPS

Talari Shanthala

Asst.Professor & IIC Conveyor, Civil Engineering Department,
Rajeev Gandhi Memorial College of Engineering and Technology, Nandyal, Andhra Pradesh, India.
shanthalas30@gmail.com

Neravati Upendra

Asst.Professor & IIC Member, Mechanical Engineering Department,
Rajeev Gandhi Memorial College of Engineering and Technology, Nandyal, Andhra Pradesh, India.

ABSTRACT

Entrepreneurship and start-ups are central to driving economic growth and fostering innovation in modern economies. This paper explores the dynamics of entrepreneurship, the lifecycle of start-ups, and the ecosystem that nurtures their growth. It examines the challenges faced by start-ups and highlights success factors through case studies. Using a mixed-method approach, this study evaluates data from emerging markets and developed economies, providing actionable insights into fostering entrepreneurial success. The findings underline the importance of innovation, resilience, and supportive ecosystems in ensuring startup sustainability.

Keywords: Entrepreneurship, Startups, Innovation, Ecosystem, Economic Growth, Emerging Markets.

THE BUSINESS OF INTELLECTUAL PROPERTY: A LITERATURE REVIEW OF IP MANAGEMENT RESEARCH

Roshni Yadav

St. Claret College Autonomous.
roshniydv00@gmail.com

ABSTRACT

Intellectual Property (IP) is pivotal in shaping modern business strategies, driving innovation, and fostering economic growth. Effective IP management ensures a competitive edge, enhances market value, and supports knowledge-driven economies. This paper presents a comprehensive literature review on IP management, focusing on its significance, strategies, challenges, and the role of legal frameworks in safeguarding intellectual assets. The review synthesizes existing research on IP valuation, commercialization, enforcement, and international implications to provide insights into best practices for businesses and policymakers.

Keywords: Intellectual Property, IP Management, Innovation, Legal Frameworks, Commercialization, Digital Protection.

LABOUR IN THE AI ERA: EMERGENCY OR ENCOURAGEMENT?

Mahadev Shivagouda Dharigoudar

Assistant Professor, KLE College of Commerce, Jakkeri Honda, Belagavi
helpmahadev@gmail.com

ABSTRACT

The rapid advancement of artificial intelligence (AI) presents both unprecedented opportunities and significant challenges for labor markets worldwide. In this context, as policymakers, it is important to pay attention to the evolving technological landscape and the potential impact it can have on the labour market. Historical parallels with earlier technological revolutions reveal the critical role of inclusive institutions in managing disruption and ensuring equitable outcomes. Barriers to large-scale AI adoption persist in the present, which include concerns over reliability, resource inefficiencies, and infrastructure deficits. These challenges, along with AI's experimental nature, create a window for policymakers to act. India's demographic advantage and diverse economic landscape position it uniquely to benefit from AI. However, achieving these benefits requires significant investments in education and workforce skilling, supported by enabling, insuring, and stewarding institutions. These mechanisms can help workers adapt to changing demands while providing essential safety nets.By fostering collaboration between policymakers, the private sector, and academia, India can align AI-driven innovation with societal goals. Ensuring inclusivity and sustainability in this transition is key to maximizing benefits while minimizing disruptions. With robust institutional frameworks and strategic planning, AI can serve not as a crisis but as a catalyst for equitable economic transformation, positioning India to thrive in an increasingly automated world.

Keywords: AI and Labor Markets, AI Adoption Challenges, Workforce Skilling, AI Policy Frameworks, Economic Transformation.

A STUDY ON THE IMPACT OF MODERN MARKETING STRATEGIES ON THE SUCCESS OF NEW PRODUCTS

Revathi. M

PhD Research Scholar (Part-Time)
Rvs College Of Arts and Science
Sulur, Coimbatore.

Dr.K. Sarulatha

Assistant Professor
School of Business Management
RVS College of Arts and Science
Sulur, Coimbatore

ABSTRACT

Modern marketing methods have changed to take use of innovative technologies and innovative strategies in the current digital world. These tactics cover a broad spectrum, such as influencer collaborations, content marketing, social media interaction, data-driven marketing, and search engine optimization (SEO). Businesses may better target certain consumers with their marketing campaigns by utilizing big data and analytics. The environment has also changed as a result of the growth of mobile marketing and customized customer experiences, which enables businesses to communicate with customers instantly. All things considered, contemporary marketing tactics emphasize developing deep, tailored connections that increase engagement and cultivate brand loyalty. The purpose of this study is to examine at the significance modern methods of marketing are to a new product's success. The potential impact of contemporary marketing techniques, such as influencer, content, loyalty, social media, and targeted email campaigns, on increasing the success rate of new goods is evaluated. The goal of the study is to show how a new product's overall performance is correlated with the use of various contemporary marketing strategies.

Keywords: Modern Marketing Strategies, Digital Marketing Techniques, Consumer Engagement, Brand Loyalty, Data-Driven Marketing.

A STUDY ON STUDENT PERCEPTION TOWARDS THE E-PAYMENT IN BANGALORE

Maria Anjali L

1st M. Com, St. Claret College,
Autonomous, Bengaluru

Mr. Manjunatha G

Assistant Professor, PG Department of Commerce, St. Claret College, Autonomous, Bengaluru.
gmanjunatha@claretcollege.edu.in

ABSTRACT

E-wallets have emerged as the most significant contributor in pushing cashless and electronic payments. E-commerce provides the capability of buying and selling products, information and services on the Internet and other online environments. In an e-commerce environment, payments take the form of money exchange in an electronic form, and are therefore called Electronic Payment. E-Payment system is secure there should be no threat to the user credit card number, smart card or other personal detail, payment can be carried out without involvement of third party, It makes E payment at any time through the internet directly to the transfer settlement and form E-business environment. Studied have been carried out on E-Payment system. E-Payment system an integral part of electronic commerce. An efficient payments system reduces the cost of exchanging goods and services, and is indispensable to the functioning of the interbank, money, and capital markets the research methodology is based on the primary data through structured questionnaire and secondary data. The main findings in this study are. New and improved methods of payments are more widely used by the younger generation due to higher level of acceptance of new technologies.

Keywords: Internet banking, electronic payment, online shopping, ease of use, security.

IMPACT OF ARTIFICIAL INTELLIGENCE ON MENTAL ACCOUNTING BEHAVIORS: INSIGHTS FROM DIGITAL PAYMENT SYSTEMS

Khuld Mahfooz

Research Scholar, Department of Management and Commerce,
Maulana Azad National Urdu University, Hyderabad

Saidalavi K

Assistant Professor, Department of Management and Commerce,
Maulana Azad National Urdu University, Hyderabad

ABSTRACT

Artificial Intelligence integrated financial tools and platforms have growing significance in shaping financial behavior. This study provides a comprehensive review of the role of artificial intelligence (AI) in influencing mental accounting behaviors within the context of digital payment systems. Mental accounting, a cognitive process wherein individuals categorize and perceive money differently based on its source or intended use, often diverges from the principle of fungibility. The research investigates how AI-driven technologies impact consumers' budgeting, spending, saving, and investment behaviors, focusing on the cognitive and behavioral nuances of mental accounting. Through an extensive review of existing literature, this study highlights the dual-edged effects of AI on financial decision-making, including the potential for improved financial management alongside challenges such as expense misclassification, diminished awareness of spending patterns, and an overreliance on algorithmic insights that may misalign with personal financial objectives. The findings offer significant practical implications, providing an understanding of the interplay between AI technologies and consumer financial behavior. This study contributes actionable recommendations for the design of AI systems that support more informed, autonomous, and responsible financial decision-making, thereby addressing critical gaps in the understanding of AI's role in consumer finance.

Keywords: Artificial Intelligence, Mental Accounting, Digital Payment Systems, behavioral finance.

ANALYZING THE EFFECTIVENESS OF CHATBOTS IN CUSTOMER SERVICE AND LEAD GENERATION

Mr. Manjunatha G

Assistant Professor, PG Department of Commerce, St. Claret College, Autonomous, Bengaluru.

Mr. Shivakumar S

1st M.Com, St. Claret College, Autonomous, Bengaluru.

ABSTRACT

The growth of e-retail was fueled by the rising use of cellphones and the Internet in emerging nations. Conversational commerce is rapidly growing through messenger-based contact. Businesses have embraced messaging chatbots in order to capitalize on both trends. These chatbots help with online purchasing using the messenger interface and provide real-time responses to customers using artificial intelligence and natural language processing. The purpose of this study is to identify the variables that impact messenger chatbot usage and how they impact attitude and behavior intention. The results from 104 respondents were gathered by the authors using an online survey, and structural equation modeling was performed. The greatest significant impact on consumer attitude has been demonstrated by customer trust, which is followed by perceived usefulness and perceived ease of use. Additionally, the employment of chatbots to speed up online purchasing has a big impact on how soon messenger chatbots will be used for online shopping. The writers examine a number of variables that lead to consumers accepting chatbots as an m-commerce interface. The results suggest that companies should create messenger chatbots as a means of enhancing consumer connection and fostering more trustworthy dialogues. An anthropomorphic digital technology-based theoretical digital marketing strategy to conversational commerce may be the subject of future research.

Keywords: Messenger Chatbots, Conversational Commerce, M-Commerce, Technology Acceptance Model, Artificial Intelligence, Online Shopping Experience, Anthropomorphism.

ROLE OF BIOTECHNOLOGY IN ENVIRONMENT BASED ENTREPRENEURSHIP

Supriyo Acharya

PG student, Department of Bioengineering & Biotechnology, BIT MESRA, Ranchi.
supriyoacharya4@gmail.com

ABSTRACT

In simple terms, biotechnology is technology that is based on biology. Biotechnology uses cellular and biomolecular processes to develop technologies and products that help improve our lives and the health of the planet. Biotechnology is not a new science. The biological processes of microorganisms have been used for thousands of years to make food like bread and cheese. Modern biotechnology uses products and technologies that increase the efficiency of food production, reduce negative impacts on the environment and use less and cleaner energy. Agricultural biotechnology refers to the use of technologies to increase crop yields, prevent damage and risks to plant and animal health and reduce the impact of farming on the environment. It involves many different types of technology and science, including breeding, genetics, synthetic chemistry and animal health. Biotechnology includes a wide range of applications. For example, it has helped make antibiotic production more efficient through microbial fermentation, which produces chemical changes in organic substrates through the action of enzymes. Farmers have long manipulated crops and animals through artificial selection to get offspring with certain traits; for example, breeding two different breeds of dairy cattle to get specific traits from both breeds. In comparison, genetic modification involves the process of incorporating new genes from one species into an unrelated species or manipulating the genetics of a species. Artificial selection selects for traits already present in a species, whereas genetic modification can create new traits. As the science of genetics is better understood, different biotechnologies are being applied to both plant and livestock agriculture. A more recent form of biotechnology is called genome editing. The word "genome" refers to the entire DNA sequence in an organism. Genome editing is precise manipulation of a plant's or animal's genetics, making specific changes to the DNA.

Keywords: Biotechnology, Genetic modification, Agricultural Biotechnology, Genome editing, Microbial fermentation.

THE IMPACT OF ARTIFICIAL INTELLIGENCE IN TRANSFORMING THE ACCOUNTING PRACTICES

Sridevi Hiremath

Lecturer in KLE's College of Commerce,
Jakkeri Honda, Belagavi.
sridevi.hiremath35@gmail.com

ABSTRACT

Artificial Intelligence (AI) is revolutionizing the accounting industry by enhancing the efficiency, accuracy, and decision-making processes. This paper explores the transformative impact of AI technologies, such as machine learning and natural language processing on accounting practices. Key findings indicate that AI improves financial forecasting, automates repetitive tasks, and strengthens fraud detection mechanisms. The study concludes by highlighting challenges and opportunities for integrating AI into accounting frameworks. Challenges in implementation, including data quality issues, workforce adaptation, and ethical considerations, are discussed. Opportunities arising from AI integration, such as enhanced decision-making, cost reduction, and strategic financial management, are highlighted through case studies. The evolving role of accountants in the AI era is examined, emphasizing a shift towards strategic interpretation and decision-making.

Keywords: Artificial Intelligence, Machine Learning, Fraud Detection, Accounting Practices, Challenges and Opportunities.

THE IMPACT OF SOCIAL MEDIA MARKETING ON BRAND AWARENESS

Sneha D

1st M. Com, St. Claret College, Autonomous, Bengaluru.

Mr. Manjunatha G

Assistant Professor, PG Department of Commerce,
St. Claret College, Autonomous, Bengaluru.
gmanjunatha@claretcollege.edu.in

ABSTRACT

Social media, an essential instrument in today's communication environment, is also evolving into an essential channel for business communication. It is being utilized by more and more businesses because of its structure, which enables direct communication between the business and its clients, and because it is more effective than traditional communication methods. Because social media usage is always growing, it is crucial to consider how new generation communication platforms affect brand recognition. For this reason, the impact of Facebook, one of the most popular social media platforms in studies (or literature), on businesses' brand recognition is looked at. According to study done on young customers in the İzmir region, social media can have a significant impact on brand awareness. Based on regression study, 34% of brand recognition can be attributed to Facebook. Accordingly, it is believed that making greater use of the benefits of social media platforms can have a major positive impact on brand awareness, and this is something that needs additional investigation.

Keywords: Social Media Use Intensity (SMUI), Social Integration and Emotional Connection (SIEC), Integration into Social Routines (ISR), Brand Awareness (BA).

VIRTUAL CONSUMERISM: IMPACT OF TECHNOLOGY ON BUYING BEHAVIOUR

Dr. Smitha. N. S

Associate Professor
Sāmbhram Academy of Management Studies
Smithans12@gmail.com

Ms. Aruna C. S

Assistant Professor
Sāmbhram Academy of Management Studies
arunasrini978@gmail.com

ABSTRACT

The rapid advancement of digital technology has significantly transformed consumer behaviour, shaping the way individuals engage with products and services. Increased internet accessibility, the influence of social media, and the rise of e-commerce have altered traditional shopping habits, making virtual consumerism an integral aspect of modern commerce. This study examines how digital transformation affects consumer decision-making, purchasing behaviour, and brand interactions. Through qualitative and quantitative research, data was collected from diverse consumer segments to analyse emerging trends. The findings indicate that digital consumers prioritize convenience, rely on online reviews, and are highly influenced by social media and targeted marketing. Additionally, the integration of artificial intelligence and big data analytics has enhanced companies' ability to predict and respond to consumer preferences. These insights provide valuable implications for businesses and marketers to develop effective digital strategies that enhance customer engagement and satisfaction in an increasingly virtual marketplace.

Keywords: Virtual consumerism, digital shopping, online behaviour, e-commerce, social media influence, artificial intelligence, consumer preferences, technology-driven marketing.

A STUDY ON THE FUTURE OF WORK: HR INNOVATIONS AND EMERGING REMOTE WORK MODELS

Dr. Champa Ramkrishna Parab

Associate Professor, Department of Commerce
MES Vasant Joshi College of Arts and Commerce, Zuarinagar, Goa
champaparab@gmail.com | 9823162461

ABSTRACT

The future of work is being reshaped by digital transformation, workforce decentralization, and HR innovations that support remote employment. This study explores the evolution of remote work models, focusing on the role of HR in driving workplace innovation and enhancing employee productivity. The research examines emerging digital platforms that facilitate remote employment across industries, assessing their impact on job accessibility, recruitment, and talent management. This study adopts an exploratory research methodology, utilizing qualitative analysis of various remote job boards, freelance marketplaces, and tech-specific employment platforms. Websites such as We Work Remotely, Remote.co, and FlexJobs provide structured remote job opportunities, while gig platforms like Upwork and Fiverr enable freelancers to connect with global clients. Additionally, tech-focused platforms like Stack Overflow Jobs, GitHub Jobs, and Dice cater to IT and programming professionals seeking remote roles. The research evaluates these platforms based on accessibility, job diversity, security, and user engagement. Key findings reveal that HR innovations, such as AI-driven recruitment, virtual collaboration tools, and digital performance tracking, have become essential for managing remote teams. The study also highlights challenges such as work-life balance, job security, and employer expectations in remote settings. These insights contribute to understanding how HR strategies can foster a more inclusive and sustainable remote work environment. The implications of this research are significant for businesses, HR professionals, and job seekers navigating the evolving job market. By leveraging digital platforms and HR technology, organizations can enhance remote workforce efficiency, attract top talent, and remain competitive in the future of work.

Keywords: Remote Work, HR Innovation, Future, Digital Platforms, Freelancing, Workforce, Recruitment.

CRYPTO CURRENCY REGULATIONS AND THEIR IMPACT ON INVESTMENT TRENDS IN INDIA

Ms. Naga Harshitha R.B

Student
Department of Management Studies, Dayananda Sagar College of Engineering
harshithabadri0@gmail.com
ORCID ID: https://orcid.org/**0009-0002-4012-967X**

Prof. Ramya H P

Assistant Professor
Department of Management Studies, Dayananda Sagar College of Engineering
ramya-mbavtu@dayanadasagar.edu
ORCID ID: https://orcid.org/0000-0002-2048-807X

ABSTRACT

Cryptocurrency is one of the most popular investment products in India that attracted retail as well as institutional investors, but the regulatory framework surrounding cryptocurrency markets remains uncertain, which creates challenges for various stakeholders. A good understanding of impacts has to be made for policy-making that encourages innovation while ensuring market stability. Since global research extensively covers the regulation of cryptocurrency, the specific policies for India remain unclear and silent about how these will be shaping investment trends. This study aims to bridge that gap by tracing the evolution of cryptocurrency regulations and how the latter will influence investor trust, trading patterns, and the overall dynamics in Indian markets through an analysis of government reports, market research, articles, and trends in cryptocurrencies. The findings depict how regulations impact investor trust and sometimes lead to a change in trading volumes and patterns. How investors preferred other platforms at times of strict policies and how transparent and stable regulations have helped more participation. It also shows the need for an equilibrist regulatory framework, which will enhance innovation but keep investors protected. This insight will offer actionable recommendations for stakeholders to adapt to the changing cryptocurrency landscape in India.

Keywords: Cryptocurrency regulations, Investment trends, Regulatory framework, Market dynamics.

HR THROUGH AI AND PEOPLE ANALYTICS: A STRATEGIC FRAMEWORK FOR WORKFORCE OPTIMIZATION

Md. Tarique Jawaid

Department of Management and Commerce
Maulana Azad National Urdu University, Hyderabad, India

Dr. Saidalavi K

Assistant Professor, Department of Management and Commerce
Maulana Azad National Urdu University, Hyderabad, India

ABSTRACT

Emerging innovations have changed the landscape of HR and posed many challenges for organizations, such as the integration of HR technology and automation with existing HR systems, lack of skills, data quality, data infrastructure, and ethical challenges in adopting AI-powered people analytics. There is a lack of understanding of leveraging AI-powered people analytics and how metaverse can be used to optimize HR functions.The objectives of this paper are to offer a comprehensive model of understanding the practices of people analytics, the application of AI-powered people analytics, and the infusion of metaverse to optimize workforce management and to explore the challenges. Further, this study seeks to explore the potential of AI-driven people analytics and metaverse and to propose a theoretical framework for understanding and leveraging people analytics, This study submits a comprehensive model for understanding the role and application of people analytics and found that AI-powered people analytics has been applied to almost every domain of HR such as talent acquisition, training and development, performance management, employee well-being, and mental health, HR strategies, and decision-making. Particularly organizations can leverage ML from data mining to processing to insights visualization. This study also highlights challenges in the adoption of AI-powered people analytics. This study offers theoretical contributions and practical implications for people analytics and provides valuable insights for researchers and HR professionals.

Key Words: AI-driven people analytics, Data-driven decision making, HR Analytics.

TALENT ACQUISITION AND RETENTION IN GLOBAL MARKET: A REVIEW ON CHALLENGES AND THE IMPACT OF LATEST INNOVATIONS IN GLOBAL TALENT MANAGEMENT

Shashikala H

Asst. Professor

S.E.A college of Science, Commerce and Arts

K.R.Puram,Bengaluru-49

ABSTRACT

In recent times, global organizations have realized the human capital as the paramount significance in any business forms. Having the right talent management plays a crucial role in building an organization. This research paper broadly examines the global talent management, in specific the challenges, innovations and their impact on talent acquisition and retention. The study analyses the complexities of talent acquisition and retention in global markets, which involves older and younger generations, skilled employees across different regions, highlighting the need for organizations to develop innovative strategic approaches to attract and retain top talent from diverse cultural backgrounds while navigating varying legal landscapes. There is a dramatic increase in the need of talent management especially hiring and retaining of the skilled employees by the multinational firms to make a mark in the competitive global world. The amalgamation of different innovations in the talent acquisition and retention greatly impacts the Human resource management. This research paper explores the transformative impact of innovative techniques that are implemented in global talent management, which directs the organization in bridging the global perspective.

Keywords: Human capital, global perspective, legal landscapes, multinational firms, innovative techniques, global talent management.

A STUDY ON THE FUTURE OF WORK: HR INNOVATIONS AND EMERGING REMOTE WORK MODELS

Dr. Champa Ramkrishna Parab

Associate Professor, Department of Commerce
MES Vasant Joshi College of Arts and Commerce, Zuarinagar, Goa
champaparab@gmail.com | 9823162461

ABSTRACT

The future of work is being reshaped by digital transformation, workforce decentralization, and HR innovations that support remote employment. This study explores the evolution of remote work models, focusing on the role of HR in driving workplace innovation and enhancing employee productivity. The research examines emerging digital platforms that facilitate remote employment across industries, assessing their impact on job accessibility, recruitment, and talent management. This study adopts an exploratory research methodology, utilizing qualitative analysis of various remote job boards, freelance marketplaces, and tech-specific employment platforms. Websites such as We Work Remotely, Remote.co, and Flex Jobs provide structured remote job opportunities, while gig platforms like Upwork and Fiverr enable freelancers to connect with global clients. Additionally, tech-focused platforms like Stack Overflow Jobs, GitHub Jobs, and Dice cater to IT and programming professionals seeking remote roles. The research evaluates these platforms based on accessibility, job diversity, security, and user engagement. Key findings reveal that HR innovations, such as AI-driven recruitment, virtual collaboration tools, and digital performance tracking, have become essential for managing remote teams. The study also highlights challenges such as work-life balance, job security, and employer expectations in remote settings. These insights contribute to understanding how HR strategies can foster a more inclusive and sustainable remote work environment. The implications of this research are significant for businesses, HR professionals, and job seekers navigating the evolving job market. By leveraging digital platforms and HR technology, organizations can enhance remote workforce efficiency, attract top talent, and remain competitive in the future of work.

Keywords: Remote Work, HR Innovation, Future, Digital Platforms, Freelancing, Workforce, Recruitment.

INNOVATION IN LOGISTICS SERVICES: A PESTLE ANALYSIS OF OUTSOURCING AND GOVERNMENTAL INFLUENCE

Ms Bandana Yadav

SHE's Sridora Caculo college of Commerce and Management studies
khorlim mapusa Goa
bandanayadav023@gmail.com

Ms. Madhumeeta Dhar

Assistant Professor, GVM College of commerce and Economics Ponda Goa
Madhumeetadhar2029@gmail.com

ABSTRACT

The logistics services sector is experiencing a revolutionary change fuelled by technological innovation, changing market needs, and policy interventions. This research investigates the function of innovation in logistics outsourcing using an extensive PESTLE analysis, addressing the political, economic, social, technological, legal, and environmental variables influencing the industry. The critical emphasis is given to the government's role in creating an environment for innovation through regulatory policies, infrastructure, and policy incentives. Based on secondary data analysis, this research analyzes major trends, challenges, and patterns of growth in logistics innovation. Through correlation and regression analysis, the study tests the relationship between government policy, investment in technology, and the efficiency of logistics outsourcing. It also establishes the influence of environmental and economic factors on the sector's development. Through the examination of new trends and strategic reactions, this study supplies evidence-based analyses for industry members to improve the efficiency, sustainability, and competitive edge of logistic services. Logistics innovation boosts the efficiency of operations, cuts costs, and increases service quality via automation, artificial intelligence, and data analytics. Through technological adoption, companies are able to build a competitive advantage, making them resilient and responsive in a fast-changing global supply chain.

Keywords: Logistics innovation, PESTLE analysis, outsourcing, government policy, technological advancement.

ARTIFICIAL INTELLIGENCE AND IT IN BUSINESS: A DATA-DRIVEN EXPLORATION OF TRANSFORMATION AND GROWTH

Dr. Deepali Gurudas Naik

Assistant Professor, Department Of Commerce.
Goa Vidyaprasarak Mandal's
Gopal Govind Poy Raiturcar College Of Commerce And Economics
Farmagudi Ponda Goa.
naikdeepali17@gmail.com, 9637214287

Ms. Madhumeeta Dhar

Assistant Professor, GVM College of Commerce and Economics Ponda Goa
Madhumeetadhar2029@gmail.com

ABSTRACT

The exponential growth in Information Technology (IT) and Artificial Intelligence (AI) has revolutionized business activities, market frameworks, and economic performance globally. This research delves into the extensive impact of IT and AI on business through the use of secondary data obtained from Internet World Stats, Digital Market Outlook and other academic sources. A thorough review of literature and documentary research approach were used in gathering relevant information, emphasizing main variables like internet penetration, digitalization, and ICT integration into business. Descriptive analysis, the research study analyzes trends in international internet usage and digitization of businesses, while statistical methods like correlation and regression are used to analyze the impact of IT adoption on business performance measures. The findings indicate the implications of AI-based decision-making, automation, and connectivity in making businesses more efficient, scalable, and competitive. The research study also examines issues like risks of cybersecurity threats, digital divide, and ethics related to AI adoption in business.Through the integration of empirical evidence and scholarly literature, this study offers a critical appreciation of how IT and AI are reshaping business environments, driving economic development, and determining future technological directions. The study's implications are far-reaching to policymakers, business executives, and researchers, providing a basis for strategic decision-making in the changing digital economy.

Keywords: IT adoption, Artificial Intelligence, Digital transformation, Business performance, Growth.

EMBRACING GREEN: BRIDGING THE GAP BETWEEN SUSTAINABLE ACTIONS TO SUSTAINABLE CONSUMPTION

Prof Sangeeta Yadav

School of Management & Commerce, Garden city University

ABSTRACT

As environment- and health-conscious consumers increasingly shift their preferences towards organic and eco-friendly lifestyles, businesses are leveraging this trend by adopting Green Production (GP) and Green Marketing (GM) strategies. Firms such as Pro Nature, 24 Mantra Organic, Down To Earth, Organic Tattva, and global brands like Zara (Inditex) have embraced sustainable practices to cater to this growing demand. This empirical study examines Green Consumption Behavioural (GCB) Trends among consumers in the metropolitan cities of Bangalore and Hyderabad, analysing their purchasing preferences and sustainability-driven choices. By identifying key drivers and barriers to Sustainable Consumption, the study offers insights into how green interventions can shape consumer behaviour and corporate sustainability strategies. The findings contribute to the broader discourse on environmental responsibility and offer actionable recommendations for businesses and policymakers aiming to foster a greener economy.

Key words: Green Marketing, Green interventions, Sustainable Consumption.

AI-DRIVEN BUSINESS MANAGEMENT: TRANSFORMING STRATEGY, INNOVATION, AND DECISION-MAKING

Ms. Shivakumari

MBA Student
Patel Institute Of Science And Management

Dr. Jeena Raju

HOD MBA Department, Patel Institute of Science and Management, Bangalore
pismjeena@gmail.com

ABSTRACT

Artificial Intelligence (AI) and Machine Learning (ML) are revolutionizing business management by enhancing strategic decision-making, improving efficiency, and fostering innovation. This conceptual study explores the transformative role of AI-driven technologies in key business functions, including strategy development, marketing, supply chain management, and customer engagement. AI enables organizations to harness large datasets, apply predictive analytics, and automate processes, leading to driven insights and improved operational agility. The study examines how AI contributes to competitive advantage by optimizing resource allocation, reducing operational costs, and enhancing customer experiences trough personalized recommendations and intelligent automation. Additionally, AI-driven business management enhances risk assessment and fraud detection, ensuring more secure and transparent operations. However, integrating AI into business processes presents challenges such as data privacy concerns, ethical implications, and workforce displacement. Addressing these challenges requires a balanced approach that combines technological advancements with human oversight and ethical AI frameworks. Furthermore, the study highlights the need for businesses to invest in AI literacy and workforce up skilling to maximize AI's potential while ensuring job roles evolve alongside technological advancements. The findings suggest that rapidly changing business environment. As AI continues to evolve, future research should focus on its long-term on leadership, decision-making and sustainable business strategies. This study provides a conceptual foundation for understanding AI's role in modern management, emphasizing both opportunities and challenges in leveraging AI and operational success.

Keywords: Artificial Intelligence, Machine Learning, Business Management, Predictive Analytics, Automation.

AI-READY MINDS- PREPAREDNESS OF THE RURAL STUDENTS FOR THE AI DRIVEN JOB SECTOR

Mr. Robin Joseph Sera

Lecturer in Commerce, Sacred Heart College, Madanthyar,
robinsera361@gmail.com

Ms. Vaishnavi Y Acharya

M.com Previous, Sacred Heart College Madanthyar,
vaishnavi.y.acharyaa@gmail.com

Ms. M J Jeena Mary

M.com Previous, Sacred Heart College Madanthyar,
jeenamarymj@gmail.com

ABSTRACT

There was a paradigm shift in the thought process of people when human labour was replaced by machines during the industrial revolution. It opened new opportunities and insights. This leads the industries to scale up the operation that is ever imagined. The labour force found the new competitor, which is more efficient and cost effective. The AI revolution forced the people to adapt the new skills and traits to escape from the 'pink slip'. The Graduates and other job seekers who hails from rural colleges are waiting to dwell into the job market are conscious about Artificial intelligence and rigorously trying to upgrade their digital skills. The Higher education and system and institutional are also not left behind in this race. The introduction of National education policy 2020 and Introduction of AI related courses in the traditional programs syllabi is a perfect exemplify the commitment to instill the AI skillset among the students. The study focuses on students at Mangalore University with aim: To assess the current state of AI Related education in the curriculum, to evaluate the effectiveness of AI skill development programs in education, to understand the perception of rural students towards AI driven Job Sector and to find the methods to incorporate in curriculum to instill the AI skills. The research involves the quantitative approaches considering the data from primary and secondary sources. The findings of the research are expected to bridge the gap between academic preparation and dynamic requirements for AI driven job sector

Keywords: AI-driven Job sector, digital skills, Artificial intelligent education National education policy 2020, skill development.

ARTIFICIAL INTELLIGENCE: MACHINE LEARNING: BLOCK CHAIN: CYBER SECURITY: IN PROCURMENT 5.0 IN SUPPLY CHAIN

Pallikkara Viswanathan

Faculty, Indian Insitute Of Materials Management, Bangalore Branch

ABSTRACT

Artificial intelligence is a new developing discipline, its potential is wide ranging and still to be fully defined, but already we can see the dramatic impact it can have on data processing, also procurement in the concept of 5.0 in supply chain. Cyber Security is said to be a subset of supply chain security, which is focused on the management of cyber security, the requirements for information, technology, systems, software networks, which are mainly driven by different aspects in supply chain, such as cyber thefts, threats, phishing, in procurement in today's world of 5.0 in supply chain. Artificial intelligence bears sourcing patterns, also the behaviors, which will be able to connect with the best suppliers more quickly, with efficiency, as it can reserve the skills, required, for the supplier selection, negotiation, bring in value assessment in the present conditions of 5.0 in supply chain. Before sourcing begins, the standard spend analysis report can now produce demand breakdown, common cost analysis, also the best supplier analysis. Armed with knowledge with about suppliers, current market conditions, procurement should then be able to run real time reports during any event such as to real down by product service carrier, cross supplier, comparison with variance, also bring outward analysis, in order to ensure that the data driven strategy on the decision, that procurement is getting the absolute deal from the sourcing process in the present condition of 5.0 in supply chain. Artificial intelligence is said to have gained as an emerging field in supply chain, with latest development, operation research, programming on various methods used with numerical analogy in supply chain. Artificial intelligence refers to have the best ability for the present machines to learn from the experiences, mainly on decisions making, better performances, consistent on being intelligent on par with human beings with a better 5.0 concept in supply chain. **Block chain** provides an efficient also viable solutions to the afore mentioned hurdles, that are restricting today's procurement in supply chain, specially it offers opportunities to synchronize process that occur within supply methods resulting in reduced cost of goods, also cash management freed from working capital in a world class of 5.0 in supply chain.

Key words: Supply chain: Artificial Intelligence: Cyber Security: Procurement: Sourcing: Cost Analysis: Suppliers: Data driven: Operation Research: Block chain.

A STUDY ON NEW INNOVATIONS IN EMPLOYEE TRAINING AND DEVELOPMENT

Anupkumar Jamboti

Assistant Professor, KLE College of Commerce, Jakkeri Honda, Belagavi.
Address: Hanuman Nagar Belagavi. Dist: Belagavi
Email: anupkumarjamboti@gmail.com

ABSTRACT

The success of organizations has historically been significantly influenced by the training and development of employees. This process equips individuals with the necessary skills and knowledge to perform effectively within their roles. The evolution of work, driven by technological advancements and changing workforce demands, has necessitated substantial adaptations in training methodologies. The present study investigates contemporary trends in employee training and development, with a particular emphasis on emerging strategies such as artificial intelligence (AI), gamification, virtual reality (VR), augmented reality (AR), and microlearning. These innovative approaches aim to deliver learning experiences that are customized, engaging, and effective in addressing diverse employee requirements. A qualitative research approach was employed, involving a comprehensive review of existing literature and case studies from organizations that have implemented these progressive strategies. It was observed that AI facilitates the creation of personalized learning trajectories, while gamification has been associated with increased motivation and active participation among employees. Furthermore, immersive technologies, including VR and AR, have demonstrated notable efficacy in sectors that require practical, hands-on training experiences. Microlearning, on the other hand, provides flexible learning opportunities that can be adapted to the varying needs of employees. The shift toward remote work has also accelerated the integration of digital platforms and Learning Management Systems (LMS), which play a critical role in maintaining consistent training experiences across geographically diverse teams. Despite the numerous advantages associated with these innovations, organizations encounter various challenges, including significant financial investments, resistance to change, and the necessity for upgraded technological infrastructures. This study critically examines the effects of these novel training methods on employee performance and engagement, as well as the obstacles that organizations must navigate to successfully implement them. The conclusion offers pragmatic recommendations aimed at optimizing the utilization of these innovations to enhance training effectiveness and foster organizational growth. The research serves as a valuable resource for organizations and human resource professionals striving to remain competitive in the continually evolving landscape of employee development.

Keywords: Employee Training, Innovations, Development, AI, Gamification, Virtual Reality, Microlearning, Employee Engagement, Organizational Growth.

IMPACT ON THE CRYPTOCURRENCY AND BLOCK CHAIN TECHNOLOGY ON THE FINANCIAL SECTOR

Prashanth K

MBA Research Scholar
Soundarya Institute of Management and Science
Email: Prashanthkrishna49@gmail.com

Abhishek KD

MBA Research Scholar
Soundarya Institute of Management and Science
Email: abhikdabhi@gmail.com

Prof. Shareef AP

Assistant Pofessor
Department of MBA
Soundarya Institute of Management and Science
Email: shareef.ap@soundaryainstitutions.in

ABSTRACT

The emergence of cryptocurrency and blockchain technology has significantly impacted the financial sector, revolutionizing traditional banking, payments, and investment mechanisms. Cryptocurrencies, such as Bitcoin and Ethereum, provide decentralized financial alternatives, reducing reliance on intermediaries and enhancing transaction efficiency. Blockchain technology ensures transparency, security, and immutability, fostering trust in digital transactions and enabling smart contracts, which automate and streamline financial agreements. The financial sector has witnessed increased adoption of blockchain in cross-border payments, asset tokenization, and decentralized finance (DeFi), offering greater financial inclusion and cost reductions. However, challenges such as regulatory uncertainty, cybersecurity risks, and scalability issues persist, influencing the integration of these technologies into mainstream financial systems. Central banks are exploring Central Bank Digital Currencies (CBDCs) to counteract the disruption posed by cryptocurrencies while leveraging blockchain benefits. This study examines the transformative impact of cryptocurrency and blockchain on the financial sector, highlighting opportunities and challenges. As financial institutions and regulators navigate this evolving landscape, the adoption of blockchain-based financial solutions is expected to reshape global finance.

Keywords: Cryptocurrency, Blockchain, Decentralized Finance (DeFi), Smart Contracts, Financial Inclusion, Digital Assets, CBDCs, Financial Regulation.

HARNESSING USER-GENERATED CONTENT [UGC]: A STRATEGIC TOOL FOR ENGAGEMENT AND BRAND LOYALTY

Manoj H C

MBA Research Scholar
Soundarya Institute Of Management And Science
EMAIL: hcmanoj47@gmail.com

Kantharaju R N

MBA Research Scholar
Soundarya Institute Of Management And Science
EMAIL: kantharajukantha2003@gmail.com

Mr. Angel Chakraborty

Assistant Professor
Department Of Mba
Soundarya Institute Of Management And Science
EMAIL: angel.chakraborty@soundaryainstitutions.in

ABSTRACT

User-generated content (UGC) has become a significant force in modern marketing, shifting the traditional marketing landscape by allowing consumers to participate directly in content creation. This research explores the role of UGC in marketing strategies, focusing on how brands leverage consumer-created content to enhance engagement, build trust, and drive brand loyalty. As social media platforms continue to grow, UGC serves as a powerful tool for marketers to connect with their audience on a more authentic level. This paper examines various forms of UGC, including reviews, social media posts, videos, and blog content, analysing their impact on consumer behaviour and decision-making processes. It also investigates the benefits and challenges associated with UGC, such as credibility, brand alignment, and content control. Furthermore, the research highlights how brands can effectively incorporate UGC into their campaigns, enhancing customer engagement and fostering a sense of community. The study concludes with recommendations for businesses seeking to integrate UGC into their marketing strategies

Keywords: User-generated content [UGC], marketing strategies, consumer engagement, brand loyalty, content marketing, consumer behaviour, digital marketing.

A CONCEPTUAL STUDY ON DIGITAL BANKING AND MOBILE PAYMENT PLATFORMS

Abhishek N D

MBA Research Scholars
Soundarya Institute of Management and Science, Bangalore -560073
abhisheknd267@gmail.com

Rakshith P S

MBA Research Scholars
Soundarya Institute of Management and Science, Bangalore -560073
rakshithps4477@gmail.com

Prof. Angel Chakraborty

Assistant Professor, Department of MBA
Soundarya Institute of Management and Science, Bangalore -560073
mail id: angel.chakraborty@soundaryainstitutions.in

ABSTRACT

The rapid evolution of digital banking and mobile payments is reshaping the global financial landscape, offering unprecedented convenience, efficiency, and financial inclusion. This paper explores the role of digital banking platforms and mobile payment solutions in driving economic growth, reducing transaction costs, and expanding financial access to underserved populations. It examines emerging trends such as AI-driven banking services, blockchain-based payments, and regulatory frameworks that influence the sector's growth. The study also highlights the challenges of cybersecurity, data privacy, and regulatory compliance that impact digital banking adoption worldwide. By analyzing case studies from various economies, this paper provides insights into the future trajectory of mobile payments and their implications for financial markets and consumer behavior. Findings revealed that digital banking and mobile payments enhance financial inclusion, reduce transaction costs, and drive economic growth, but face challenges in cybersecurity, data privacy, and regulatory compliance.

Key Words: Digital Banking, Mobile Payments, Financial Inclusion, FinTech Innovation, Regulatory Compliance.

QUANTUM-ENHANCED AI: TRANSFORMING MACHINE LEARNING WITH QUANTUM COMPUTING

Sangeetha B R

MBA Research Scholar
Soundarya Institute of Management and Science
Email: sangeethabr242@gmail.com

Sandhya S

MBA Research Scholar
Soundarya Institute of Management and Science
Email: sandhyassandhyas72@gmail.com

Prof. Angel Chakraborty

Assistant Professor
Department Of MBA
Soundarya Institute of Management and Science
Email: angel.chakraborty@soundaryainstitutions.in

ABSTRACT

The convergence of quantum computing and artificial intelligence (AI) is poised to revolutionize machine learning by exponentially accelerating computations and optimizing complex algorithms. This research explores the impact of quantum computing on deep learning, reinforcement learning and data security, highlighting key breakthroughs, challenges and future directions. We studied quantum-enhanced models, quantum-inspired algorithms and their implications across industries such as healthcare, finance and cybersecurity. Our findings suggest that hybrid quantum-classical AI systems could redefine computational efficiency, paving the way for next-generation intelligent systems.

Keywords: Quantum AI, Quantum Machine Learning, Hybrid Quantum-Classical Systems, Quantum Computing, Deep Learning Optimization, Quantum Algorithms, AI Acceleration.

EXPLORING CUSTOMER PERCEPTION OF WEB ANALYSIS AND ONLINE BEHAVIOUR TRACKING IN A SURVEY-BASED APPROVAL

Shivaganesh K

Student, Department of MBA
Soundarya Institution of Management and science
Shivaganesh2046@gmail.com

Sushmitha N

Student, Department of MBA
Soundarya Institution of Management and science
sushmithan173@gmail.com

Yuvaraj Halage

Assistant Professor & coordinator
Department of MBA
Soundarya institution of Management and Science
Wisdom.yuvaraj@gmail.com

ABSTRACT

This study explores customer perceptions of web analytics and online behavior tracking through a survey-based approach. As businesses increasingly rely on digital tools for customer engagement, understanding how customers perceive these data-driven practices is critical for enhancing customer trust and improving marketing strategies. The primary objective of this research is to examine customer attitudes towards the use of web analytics and behavior tracking techniques, including concerns about privacy, personalization, and overall experience. A structured survey was administered to a sample of online consumers, with a focus on measuring their awareness, perceptions, and acceptance of tracking technologies used by websites for data collection and targeted marketing. The research findings indicate that while customers generally recognize the benefits of personalization enabled by web analytics, concerns regarding data privacy and security remain prevalent. Perceived transparency and control over personal data significantly influence customers' willingness to engage with websites employing such technologies. The study suggests that businesses should adopt transparent data collection practices, prioritize consumer consent, and communicate data protection efforts to enhance customer trust and engagement. Future research should explore the impact of demographic factors on customer perceptions and the role of trust-building mechanisms in influencing the adoption of behavior tracking technologies.

Keywords: Web Analytics, Online Behavior Tracking, Customer Perception, Data Privacy, Digital Marketing.

THE IMPACT OF SOCIAL MEDIA INFLUENCERS ON CONSUMER PURCHASING BEHAVIOR: A COMPARATIVE STUDY OF URBAN AND RURAL CONSUMERS

Sahana A

Student
Department of MBA
Soundarya Institute of Management and Science
sahanaanandaiah@gmail.com

Lohith K S

Student
Department of MBA
Soundarya Institute of Management and Science
lohithks2003@gmail.com

Yuvaraj Halage

Assistant Professor & Coordinator
Department of MBA
Soundarya Institute of Management and Science
wisdom.yuvaraj@gmail.com

ABSTRACT

This study investigates the impact of social media influencers on consumer purchasing behavior, with a comparative analysis between urban and rural consumers. The primary objective is to explore how social media influencers affect purchasing decisions and the role of consumer demographics in moderating these effects. Specifically, this research seeks to examine the differences in consumer behavior based on geographic location (urban vs. rural) and the type of influence exerted by social media personalities. Using a structured survey, data were collected from 600 consumers, equally divided between urban and rural regions, to assess their exposure to social media influencers, perceived credibility, and subsequent purchase intentions. The research employs a **multivariate analysis of variance (MANOVA)** to compare the effects of influencer-driven marketing across different consumer groups. Additionally, **regression analysis** was conducted to identify the relationship between influencer characteristics (e.g., trustworthiness, relatability) and consumer purchasing behavior. The results reveal that social media influencers significantly affect purchasing behavior, with a stronger influence observed among urban consumers who engage more frequently with influencers. In contrast, rural consumers exhibit less engagement but respond positively to influencers who promote products related to lifestyle and local relevance. Furthermore, trust and relatability were found to be critical factors influencing the effectiveness of influencer marketing. These findings offer valuable insights for marketers targeting diverse consumer segments. Future research should investigate the long-term effects of influencer marketing on brand loyalty and the ethical implications of influencer endorsements.

Keywords: Social Media Influencers, Consumer Purchasing Behavior, Urban vs. Rural Consumers, MANOVA, Regression Analysis, Marketing Strategy.

ASSESSING EMPLOYEES PERCEPTIONS OF GAMIFICATION IN HR: EASE OF USE & PERCEIVED USEFULNESS

Shwetha B

Student
Department of MBA
Soundarya Institution of Management and science
Shwethag395@gmail.com

Vinod H. A

Student
Department of MBA
Soundarya Institution of Management and science
Vinodvinu3123@gmail.com

Yuvaraj Halage

Assistant Professor & coordinator
Department of MBA
Soundarya institution of Management and Science
wisdom.yuvaraj@gmail.com

ABSTRACT

This study investigates employees' perceptions of gamification in Human Resource Management (HRM), focusing on two key factors: perceived ease of use and perceived usefulness. The primary objective is to assess how these factors influence employees' willingness to adopt gamified HR systems, particularly in areas such as performance management and training. Grounded in the Technology Acceptance Model (TAM), the research uses a quantitative approach, surveying 400 employees from various industries using a stratified random sampling method to ensure a diverse participant pool. The survey evaluates employees' attitudes towards gamified applications, specifically measuring ease of use, perceived usefulness, and adoption intention. Statistical analysis was conducted using multiple regression to examine the relationship between perceived ease of use, perceived usefulness, and willingness to adopt gamification. Additionally, Structural Equation Modelling (SEM) was employed to test the theoretical framework, while factor analysis was utilized to identify underlying factors influencing perceptions of gamification. The results reveal that perceived usefulness strongly influences the adoption of gamified HR systems, especially in training and performance management. Additionally, ease of use was found to significantly impact positive employee attitudes, indicating that intuitive, user-friendly designs increase acceptance. However, challenges such as resistance to change and unfamiliarity with gamification were identified as barriers to successful implementation. These findings offer valuable insights for HR professionals aiming to design effective gamified systems that enhance employee engagement and productivity. Future research should explore industry-specific variations and longitudinal impacts of gamification in HRM.

Keywords: Gamification, Human Resource Management, Technology Acceptance Model, Perceived Usefulness, Perceived Ease of Use, Employee Engagement.

EXPLORING THE INFLUENCE OF CORPORATE SOCIAL RESPONSIBILITY ON BRAND IMAGE AND CONSUMER PERCEPTION

Ms. Chaithra N

Research Scholar, Department of MBA,
Soundarya Institute Of Management And Science
cchaithran698@gmail.com

Mr. Rajesh I N

Research Scholar, Department of MBA,
Soundarya Institute Of Management And Science
rajeshin2003@gmail.com

Dr. Roopa Shettigar

Associate Professor, Department of MBA,
Soundarya Institute Of Management And Science
roopashettigar@soundaryainstitutions.in

Abstract

Corporate social responsibility has become a vital tactic for companies looking to improve the perception of their brands. With an emphasis on customer perception, trust, and loyalty, this study investigates the connection between CSR actions and company reputation. This study examines how socially conscious company practices affect long-term success and brand equity by examining case studies and existing research. According to the research, CSR enhances stakeholder connections and brand reputation, giving businesses a competitive edge. Companies that successfully include CSR in their plans see improvements in customer loyalty, brand distinction, and consumer trust. To maximize the impact of CSR activities, the paper's conclusion emphasizes the importance of matching them with stakeholder expectations and business values.

Keywords: Corporate Social Responsibility, Brand Reputation, Consumer Trust, Brand Equity, Stakeholder Engagement, Sustainable Business Practices.

DECODING EMPLOYEE MINDSETS: HOW AI AND NLP RESHAPE WORKPLACE CULTURE

Dr. Vasu B.A

Professor And Director
Soundarya Institute Of Management And Science, Bengaluru-560073
sims.principal@soundayainstitutions.in

Monica J

MBA Research Scholars
Soundarya Institute Of Management And Science, Bengaluru-560073
monica9629j@gmail.com

Yogashree R

MBA Research Scholars
Soundarya Institute Of Management And Science, Bengaluru-560073
yogashreer26@gmail.com

ABSTRACT

In today's dynamic work environment, understanding employee sentiments is crucial for fostering a positive workplace culture and enhancing engagement. Traditional HR methods, such as surveys and feedback sessions, often fail to capture real-time emotions and implicit sentiments. This research explores how Artificial Intelligence (AI) and Natural Language Processing (NLP) revolutionize sentiment analysis in HR by providing data-driven insights into employee mindsets. AI-powered tools analyze emails, chats, and feedback, enabling HR professionals to identify patterns, address concerns proactively, and improve overall job satisfaction. By leveraging machine learning algorithms, organizations can foster a more inclusive and responsive work environment. This paper also highlights the ethical considerations and challenges of AI-driven sentiment analysis, emphasizing the need for transparency and data privacy. The findings demonstrate how AI and NLP empower HR decision-making, transforming workplace culture into one that prioritizes employee well-being and productivity. The study provides valuable insights for businesses aiming to integrate AI in HR strategies to boost workforce morale and retention.

Keywords: Sentiment Analysis, Artificial Intelligence, Natural Language Processing, Employee Engagement, Workplace Culture.

DECODING WORKFORCE BEHAVIOUR: LEVERAGING DIGITAL FOOTPRINTS FOR PREDICTIVE HR ANALYTICS

Bhuvana J

MBA Research scholar
Soundarya Institute Of Management And Science, Bengaluru-560073
bhuvanajnaik@gmail.com

Shashikala L

MBA Research scholar
Soundarya Institute Of Management And Science, Bengaluru-560073
shashikalashashikala32698@gmail.com

Angel Chakraborty

Assistant professor,Deaprtment of MBA
Soundarya Institute Of Management And Science, Bengaluru-560073
Angel.chakraborty@soundaryainstitutions.in

ABSTRACT

In the digital era, employees generate vast amounts of data through their workplace interactions, emails, collaboration tools, and online behaviour. This study explores how organizations can leverage these digital footprints to decode workforce behaviour and enhance predictive HR analytics. By analyzing structured and unstructured data, HR professionals can gain insights into employee engagement, productivity, job satisfaction, and potential attrition risks. The research examines advanced analytical techniques, including machine learning, natural language processing (NLP), and sentiment analysis, to identify patterns and trends in workforce dynamics. Ethical considerations, including data privacy, consent, and bias mitigation, are also discussed to ensure responsible use of employee data. The study presents case studies of organizations successfully implementing digital footprint analytics and their impact on HR decision-making. Findings suggest that predictive HR analytics can optimize talent management, improve workforce planning, and foster a data-driven HR culture. However, balancing employee privacy with organizational insights remains a key challenge. This research contributes to the growing field of HR technology by providing a framework for ethical and effective use of digital footprints in workforce analytics.

Keywords: Predictive HR analytics, digital footprints, workforce behaviour, people analytics, sentiment analysis, employee engagement, data privacy.

ENTREPRENEURSHIP IN THE GIG ERA: A NEW BUSINESS MODEL

Nitheesh B S

6th semester BBA
Soundarya Institute of Management and Science
bsnitheesh4@gmail.com

ABSTRACT

A new generation of entrepreneurs marked by flexibility, digital connectedness, and on-demand services has emerged as a result of the gig economy's transformation of conventional employment structures. This study examines how independent workers use technology to develop scalable business models as it relates to entrepreneurship in the gig economy. Gigbased companies, compared to traditional organizations, rely on platforms, networks, and digital tools to reach markets and clients throughout the world with little infrastructure. In the contemporary economy, this change has redefined risk-taking, financial independence, and business sustainability. This paper focuses on the distinct obstacles and prospects that entrepreneurs encounter in the gig economy, such as fluctuating revenue, unclear regulations, and the absence of employee benefits. It also emphasizes new business models that are arising in response to these issues, like digital freelancing, platform-based entrepreneurship, and subscription-based services. The long-term sustainability of gig-driven entrepreneurship and its effects on financial wellness, job creation, and economic growth are assessed in this study The outcomes help to clarify how the gig economy creates a new type of entrepreneur, changing conventional business models and setting foundations for a more flexible and agile economy.

Keywords: Gig economy, Entrepreneurship, Business models, financial independence, Economic growth.

THE ADOPTION OF DISTRIBUTED LEDGER TECHNOLOGY IN BANKING AND FINANCE: REGULATORY CHALLENGES AND EFFICIENCY OPPORTUNITIES

Hariprasad Nayak

MBA Research Scholars
Soundarya Institute of Management and Science, Bangalore -560073
hariprasadnayak777@gmail.com

Chandra shekhar

MBA Research Scholars
Soundarya Institute of Management and Science, Bangalore -560073
chandukumbar16@gmail.com

G Vasanth kumar

Assistant Professor, Department of MBA
Soundarya Institute of Management and Science, Bangalore -560073
vasanthkumar.g@soundaryainstitutions.in

ABSTRACT

Blockchain technology has emerged as a transformative force in the financial sector, offering enhanced security, transparency, and efficiency in transactions. This paper explores the adoption of blockchain in financial services, examining its potential to revolutionize banking, payments, lending, and asset management. A quantitative analysis of 150 financial institutions adopting blockchain solutions reveals a 32% reduction in transaction costs ($p < 0.01$) and a 45% improvement in settlement speed ($p < 0.05$) compared to traditional systems. While blockchain presents numerous opportunities, such as cost reduction and improved security, its widespread adoption faces significant challenges, including regulatory uncertainty, scalability issues, and resistance from traditional institutions (Smith & Jones, 2022). Moreover, survey data from industry professionals indicate that 67% of financial executives believe regulatory hurdles are the primary barrier to blockchain implementation (Doe et al., 2023). Through an analysis of existing literature and case studies, this study highlights both the potential and limitations of blockchain adoption in finance. The findings suggest that while blockchain has the capability to reshape financial services, its success depends on overcoming technical, legal, and institutional barriers. The paper concludes with recommendations for policymakers, financial institutions, and technology developers to foster a more seamless integration of blockchain in financial systems.

Keywords: Blockchain Technology, Financial Services, Digital Transactions, Regulatory Challenges, Financial Innovation.

ASSESSING THE IMPACT OF HUMAN RESOURCE POLICIES ON WOMEN'S CAREER PROGRESSION IN THE INDIAN CONTEXT

Priyanka Y A

Student, First Year MBA,
Soundarya Institute of Management and Science, Bengaluru.

Sakshi

Student, First Year MBA,
Soundarya Institute of Management and Science, Bengaluru.

Vaibhav S Arwade

Assistant Professor, Department of MBA,
Soundarya Institute of Management and Science, Bengaluru.

ABSTRACT

This research paper examines the impact of Human Resource (HR) policies on the career development of women in India. The study investigates key HR practices, such as recruitment, performance evaluation, work-life balance initiatives, and promotion opportunities, and their influence on women's professional growth. A quantitative research method was adopted, involving 350 respondents across various industries, including IT, healthcare, education, and finance. Statistical tools such as SPSS, regression analysis, and ANOVA were employed to analyze the data. The results indicate that gender-sensitive HR policies, flexible work arrangements, and mentorship programs significantly enhance career progression for women. Conversely, discriminatory practices and inadequate maternity support were identified as major obstacles. The study concludes with recommendations for organizations to adopt inclusive HR strategies that promote equal opportunities for women.

Keywords: HR Policies, Women Career Development, Indian Workforce, Gender Equality, Work-life Balance, Employee Inclusion.

IMPACT OF PREDICTIVE ANALYTICS ON CUSTOMER BEHAVIOR AND ENGAGEMENT IN "BALANCING FLEXIBILITY AND BURNOUT: THE PSYCHOLOGICAL EFFECTS OF REMOTE WORK"

Ganika B K

Student, Department of MBA
Soundarya Institute of Management and Science
Email: gaganabk26@gmail.com

Gagana B K

Student, Department of MBA
Soundarya Institute of Management and Science
Email: ganikagowda26@gmail.com

G Vasanth Kumar

Assistant Professor, Department of MBA
Soundarya Institute of Management and Science

ABSTRACT

Remote work has transformed traditional workplace dynamics, offering employees greater flexibility while also presenting challenges such as burnout, isolation, and blurred work-life boundaries. This study examines the psychological effects of remote work, with a focus on the trade-off between flexibility and burnout. While remote work enables autonomy, reduced commute stress, and personalized work environments, it also contributes to longer working hours, digital exhaustion, and decreased social interaction (Eurofound, 2020). Using a mixed methods approach, this research analyzes employee well-being through survey data, case studies, and psychological assessments. Findings indicate that effective boundary-setting, employer support, and digital wellness strategies can mitigate the negative effects of remote work (Bloom et al., 2015). The study highlights best practices such as asynchronous communication, mental health interventions, and flexible scheduling to promote a healthier remote work culture. The research concludes that while remote work offers unparalleled flexibility, its sustainability depends on structured policies, leadership adaptability, and employee resilience-building measures (Gajendran & Harrison, 2007).

Keywords: Remote Work, Burnout, Flexibility, Work-Life Balance, Digital Fatigue, Employee Well-Being, Hybrid Work.

RISK MANAGEMENT IN GLOBAL MARKETS: STRATEGIES FOR FINANCIAL STABILITY AND COMPETITIVE RESILIENCE

Gagana BK

Student, Department of MBA
Soundarya Institute of Management and Science
Email: gaganabk26@gmail.com

Santhosh

Student, Department of MBA
Soundarya Institute of Management and Science
Email: santhoshgowda0466@gmail.com

Angel Chakraborty

Assistant Professor, Department of MBA
Soundarya Institute of Management and Science
Email: angel.chakraborty@soundaryainstitutions.in

ABSTRACT

In an increasingly interconnected global economy, risk management in global markets has become critical for businesses, investors, and policymakers. This study explores the types of risks faced in global markets, including currency fluctuations, geopolitical instability, regulatory changes, and economic crises (Brigham & Ehrhardt, 2022). It examines the effectiveness of financial instruments such as hedging, derivatives, and diversification strategies in mitigating these risks (Hull, 2018). Using a comparative analysis of multinational corporations (MNCs) and emerging market firms, the study evaluates the role of data analytics, artificial intelligence, and scenario planning in modern risk assessment. Furthermore, the research highlights the application of statistical and econometric tools such as R, Python, and MATLAB in developing predictive models, stress testing frameworks, and real-time risk simulations. The findings suggest that proactive risk management frameworks, dynamic hedging strategies, and adaptive business models enhance resilience in volatile global markets (Jorion, 2007). This research contributes to the understanding of how firms can develop robust risk mitigation strategies by leveraging data-driven insights and computational techniques to maintain financial stability and competitive advantage in an uncertain global landscape.

Keywords: Global Markets, Risk Management, Hedging, Financial Derivatives, Economic Volatility, Geopolitical Risks, Corporate Resilience, Data Analytics, Econometric Modeling.

SUSTAINABLE INNOVATIONS AND MARKET TRENDS: A PATH TO FUTURE GROWTH

Ms. Sushma N

Research Scholar, Department of MBA,
Soundarya Institute Of Management And Science.
sushmanagraj2@gmail.com

Ms. Varsha J

Research Scholar, Department of MBA,
Soundarya Institute Of Management And Science.
varshajaishankar06@gmail.com

Dr. Roopa Shettigar

Associate Professor, Department of MBA,
Soundarya Institute Of Management And Science
roopashettigar@soundaryainstitutions.in

ABSTRACT

In the contemporary era of rapid technological advancement and evolving consumer demands, sustainable innovations have emerged as a critical factor in driving market expansion. Organizations worldwide are increasingly integrating sustainability into their innovative strategies to enhance competitiveness, adhere to regulatory requirements, and address global environmental challenges. This research examines the intersection of sustainability and market trends, analyzing how enterprises implement environmentally conscious practices, circular economy principles, and green technologies to ensure long-term viability. It investigates key factors influencing sustainable innovations, including regulatory frameworks, consumer preferences, and technological advancements. Furthermore, the study presents industry case studies that illustrate the impact of sustainable business models on market dynamics. By comprehending the relationship between sustainability and emerging market trends, organizations can develop resilient strategies that promote economic growth while supporting environmental and social welfare.

Keywords: Sustainability, Innovation, Market Trends, Green Technologies, Circular Economy, Business Growth.

BEYOND CONVERSATIONS: HOW AI-POWERED CHATBOTS REDEFINE CUSTOMER EXPERIENCE

Bhavya M T

MBA Research Scholar, Soundarya Institute of Management & Science
Email: bhavyamt2907@gmail.com

Jeevitha V

MBA Research Scholar , Soundarya Institute of Management & Science
Email: jeevithav01@gmail.com

Prof. Shareef A P

Assistant Professor
Department of MBA, Soundarya Institute of Management & Science
Email: shareef.ap@soundaryainstitutions.in

ABSTRACT

The rise of AI-powered chatbots is revolutionizing customer experience by enhancing efficiency, personalization, and accessibility. These intelligent virtual assistants leverage Natural Language Processing (NLP) and Machine Learning (ML) to understand customer queries, provide instant responses, and continuously improve their interactions. Unlike traditional customer service methods, AI chatbots offer 24/7 availability, reducing wait times and improving customer satisfaction. One of the key benefits of AI-driven chatbots is their ability to personalize interactions by analysing customer data, preferences, and past interactions. This enables them to provide tailored recommendations, predictive assistance, and seamless omnichannel support. Additionally, businesses can scale customer service operations without significantly increasing costs, making chatbots a cost-effective solution. Furthermore, AI chatbots enhance engagement by integrating with various digital platforms such as websites, mobile apps, and social media. They facilitate real-time problem-solving, automate repetitive tasks, and free up human agents to handle more complex inquiries. Advanced chatbots equipped with sentiment analysis can even detect customer emotions and adjust responses accordingly, fostering stronger relationships.Despite these advantages, challenges such as data privacy concerns, lack of emotional intelligence, and limitations in handling complex queries persist. However, continuous advancements in AI are addressing these issues, making chatbots more human-like and context-aware. This paper explores the evolution, effectiveness, and challenges of AI-powered chatbots in enhancing customer experience. By evaluating their impact across industries and discussing future trends, it provides insights into how businesses can leverage AI-driven solutions to achieve higher efficiency, improved customer satisfaction, and long-term competitive advantage.

Keywords: AI Chatbots, Customer Service, Artificial Intelligence, Natural Language Processing, Machine Learning, Customer Experience, Digital Transformation.

EXPLORING CUSTOMER BEHAVIOR AND PROFITABILITY: A SURVEY ON HOW MARKETING ANALYTICS INFLUENCES CUSTOMER AND MARKETING BEHAVIOR IN BUSINESS VENTURES

Akshay kumar G N

MBA Research Scholar, Soundarya Institute of Management & Science
akshaykumarn2002@gmail.com

Madhusudhan D

MBA Research Scholar, Soundarya Institute of Management & Science
akshaykumarn2002@gmail.com

Yuvaraj Halage

Assistant Professor & Coordinator
Department of MBA
Soundarya Institute of Management and Science
wisdom.yuvaraj@gmail.com

Abstract

This study explores the relationship between marketing analytics, customer behavior, and business profitability, aiming to assess how marketing analytics influence customer decision-making and overall marketing strategies in business ventures. The primary objective is to examine how the application of marketing analytics impacts customer purchasing behavior, customer engagement, and marketing campaign effectiveness, with a focus on understanding how these factors contribute to increased profitability for businesses. Using a survey-based methodology, the research collected data from 484 customers across multiple industries who have interacted with marketing campaigns influenced by data analytics. A stratified random sampling technique was employed to ensure diverse customer representation. The data were analyzed using regression analysis to examine the correlation between marketing analytics application and changes in customer behavior, and Structural Equation Modeling (SEM) to test the relationships between customer behavior, marketing activities, and profitability. The findings suggest that marketing analytics significantly enhance customer targeting, which leads to higher engagement and improved customer loyalty, thereby increasing business profitability. Specifically, predictive analytics and customer segmentation were found to be the most influential factors in shaping customer purchasing decisions and driving marketing effectiveness. However, challenges in data interpretation and customer privacy concerns were identified as barriers to the full utilization of marketing analytics. These results provide valuable insights for businesses looking to optimize their marketing strategies using data-driven approaches. Future research should explore the long-term impact of marketing analytics on customer loyalty and profitability, as well as examine sector-specific variations and ethical considerations in data usage.

Keywords: Marketing Analytics, Customer Behavior, Profitability, Regression Analysis, Structural Equation Modeling, Customer Engagement.

THE ROLE OF BUSINESS ANALYTICS IN ENHANCING FINANCIAL DECISION-MAKING

Manoj Kumar S

MBA Research Scholar, Soundarya Institute of Management & Science
manojkumar6teen@gmail.com

Manoj B

MBA Research Scholar, Soundarya Institute of Management & Science
manojsandyvr46@gmail.com

Yuvaraj Halage

Assistant Professor & Coordinator
Department of MBA
Soundarya Institute of Management and Science
wisdom.yuvaraj@gmail.com

ABSTRACT

In the era of digital transformation and data-driven business environments, financial decision-making is undergoing a significant shift from traditional approaches to modern, analytical methodologies. Business analytics has emerged as a critical tool that empowers organizations to make well-informed, strategic, and evidence-based financial decisions. This research paper aims to explore the pivotal role of business analytics in enhancing financial decision-making by integrating data-driven insights into financial processes such as budgeting, forecasting, investment evaluation, risk assessment, and performance measurement. Business analytics encompasses a wide range of techniques, including descriptive, predictive, and prescriptive analytics, which help organizations interpret historical data, forecast future trends, and recommend optimal financial strategies. Through the application of advanced analytical tools and technologies, financial professionals can identify patterns, mitigate risks, and make accurate and timely decisions that align with business goals. Moreover, real-time analytics and artificial intelligence have further enhanced the capability of finance teams to respond quickly to market fluctuations and business challenges. This paper also highlights the significance of financial modeling, business intelligence, and dashboard reporting in improving transparency, accountability, and overall financial efficiency. By bridging the gap between traditional finance practices and modern analytical approaches, this study emphasizes the growing importance of data analytics as a catalyst for sustainable financial performance and strategic growth. The integration of business analytics into finance not only supports better decision-making but also fosters innovation, competitiveness, and long-term value creation for organizations in a highly competitive global economy.

Keywords: Business Analytics, Financial Decision-Making, Predictive Analytics, Descriptive Analytics, Prescriptive Analytics, Financial Modeling.

SUSTAINABILITY IN BUSINESS: STRATEGIES FOR LONG-TERM SUCCESS AND ENVIRONMENTAL RESPONSIBILITY

Mr. Mahabaleshwar N Hegde

MBA Research Scholar, Soundarya Institute of Management & Science
mnhegde2001@gmail.com

Mr. Karthik G

MBA Research Scholar, Soundarya Institute of Management & Science
karsmash007@gmail.com

Dr. Roopa Shettigar

Associate Professor, Department of MBA,
Soundarya Institute of Management and Science
roopashettigar@soundaryainstitutions.in

Abstract

Sustainability has emerged as a major area of concern for companies trying to strike a balance between social and environmental responsibility and economic success. The impact of sustainable business practices on improving long-term resilience, brand reputation, and company performance is examined in this essay. It looks at the advantages and difficulties of putting sustainability methods like green innovation, ethical supply chain management, and corporate social responsibility (CSR) into practice. The research examines strategic frameworks and best practices that lead to a more sustainable future through case studies from a range of businesses. According to the study's findings, sustainability is not just a moral need but also a competitive advantage that promotes long-term corporate success, regulatory compliance, and stakeholder confidence.

Keywords: Sustainability, Corporate Social Responsibility, Green Innovation, Ethical Business Practices, Sustainable Supply Chains, Environmental Responsibility.

REMOTE WORK AND ITS INFLUENCE ON EMPLOYEE PRODUCTIVITY AND MENTAL WELL-BEING

Ms. Thanuja A M

MBA Research Scholar, Soundarya Institute of Management & Science
thanujathanuja72551@gmail.com

Ms. Chaithanya T R

MBA Research Scholar, Soundarya Institute of Management & Science
chaithanyatr24@gmail.com

Dr. Roopa Shettigar

Associate Professor, Department of MBA,
Soundarya Institute of Management and Science
roopashettigar@soundaryainstitutions.in

ABSTRACT

The transition to remote work has changed the conventional workplace and had an effect on workers' mental health and productivity. The benefits and drawbacks of working remotely are examined in this study, along with how work-life balance, flexibility, and digital communication affect worker performance. Remote work has benefits like increased autonomy and less stress from commuting, but it also has drawbacks like social isolation, diversions, and trouble staying motivated. This study assesses tactics that companies can use to maximise remote work settings, guaranteeing high productivity and worker well-being, through an analysis of case studies and current literature. According to the findings, maintaining employee engagement and productivity in virtual work environments requires clear remote work policies, technology assistance, and mental health programs.

Keywords: Remote Work, Employee Productivity, Work-Life Balance, Mental Well-being, Digital Communication, Workplace Flexibility.

LEVERAGING CUSTOMER LIFETIME VALUE(LTV) ANALYTICS FOR SUSTAINABLE GROWTH IN FINTECH

Ms. Girija M

MBA Research Scholar, Soundarya Institute of Management & Science
girijam802@gmail.com

Ms. Vinutha

MBA Research Scholar, Soundarya Institute of Management & Science
vinuthadevadiga6@gmail.com

Dr. Roopa Shettigar

Associate Professor, Department of MBA,
Soundarya Institute of Management and Science
roopashettigar@soundaryainstitutions.in

ABSTRACT

Understanding and maximising Customer Lifetime Value (LTV) is crucial for achieving sustainable growth in the rapidly evolving Fintech landscape. This paper explores how Fintech companies can leverage LTV analytics to enhance customer retention, optimize marketing strategies, and drive long-term profitability. By integrating advanced data analytics, machine learning models, and behavioural insights, firms can predict customer behaviours, personalize financial offerings, and improve decision-making. Additionally, the study highlights key challenges in LTV measurement and provides strategic recommendations for Fintech firms to create sustainable and customer-centric business models. The findings emphasize that a datadriven approach to LTV not only boosts revenue but also strengthens customer relationships and brand loyalty in the competitive Fintech ecosystem..

Keywords: Customer Lifetime Value, Fintech Analytics, Sustainable Growth, Customer Retention, Data-Driven Decision Making, Financial Technology.

TECHNOLOGICAL INNOVATIONS IN LOGISTICS AND TRANSPORTATION: ENHANCING EFFICIENCY, SUSTAINABILITY, AND GLOBAL TRADE

Ganika BK

Student
Department of MBA
Soundarya Institute of Management of Science

Hemanth

Student
Department of MBA
Soundarya Institute of Management and Science

Angel Chakraborty

Assistant Professor
Department of MBA
Soundarya Institute of Management and Science

ABSTRACT

The rapid advancement of technology has transformed the logistics and transportation sector, driving efficiency, sustainability, and cost-effectiveness. This study explores key innovations in logistics and transportation, including artificial intelligence (AI), blockchain, Internet of Things (IoT), digital twins, and autonomous vehicles, and their impact on supply chain optimization and global trade (Christopher, 2016). The research highlights the role of predictive analytics and machine learning in demand forecasting, route optimization, and inventory management (Tang & Veelenturf, 2019). Additionally, the study examines green logistics initiatives, such as electrification of fleets, smart warehousing, and last-mile delivery innovations, which contribute to reducing carbon footprints and enhancing operational efficiency (Rodrigue, 2020). The integration of statistical and econometric tools such as R, Python, and MATLAB enables real time analysis of logistics performance, risk management, and cost-reduction strategies. Findings suggest that while technological innovations enhance agility and sustainability, challenges related to infrastructure, cybersecurity, and regulatory compliance remain significant barriers. The studyb concludes by proposing a strategic framework for businesses to adopt data-driven logistics solutions, ensuring long-term resilience and competitiveness in a dynamic global market.

Keywords: Logistics Innovation, Smart Transportation, Digital Twins, AI in Supply Chain, Green Logistics, Autonomous Vehicles, Blockchain in Logistics.

RETENTION REVOLUTION: HARNESSING POWER BI FOR ATTRITION ANALYTICS AND SUSTAINABLE WORKFORCE SUCCESS

Vaishnavi V

MBA Research Scholar, Soundarya Institute of Management Science
Email: vaishnavigowda6057@gmail.com

Deepthi S S

MBA Research Scholar, Soundarya Institute of Management Science
Email: deepthiss944@gmail.com

Prof. Vaibhav S Arwade

Assistant Professor Department of MBA,
Soundarya Institute of Management Science
Email: vaibhavarwade@soundaryainstitutions.in

ABSTRACT

As organizations navigate the complexities of a rapidly evolving workforce, **employee attrition** remains a critical challenge, impacting productivity, morale, and business continuity. Traditional retention strategies often fall short due to their reactive nature, necessitating a **data-driven revolution** in workforce management. This research introduces **Power BI-driven attrition analytics** as a game-changer, enabling **real-time insights, predictive modelling, and strategic interventions** for sustainable workforce success. The study aims to **decode attrition trends through Power BI**, leveraging **dynamic dashboards, data visualization, and AI-powered analytics** to identify high-risk employees and **forecast turnover patterns**. By integrating key HR metrics—including **job satisfaction, compensation trends, career progression, and work-life balance**—this research demonstrates how HR professionals can **transition from intuition-based decision-making to evidence-backed workforce strategies**. A structured methodology is adopted, utilizing **historical workforce data** to develop **interactive attrition heatmaps, risk prediction models, and performance-impact assessments** in Power BI. The study reveals that **salary stagnation, limited career mobility, and disengagement** are primary attrition drivers, while predictive analytics significantly **enhance talent retention strategies**. Findings suggest that organizations that integrate **Power BI into HR analytics** gain a **competitive edge** by transforming passive HR reports into **actionable intelligence**. This study underscores the **power of business intelligence in redefining workforce sustainability**, making attrition analytics **not just a diagnostic tool, but a strategic asset** in modern HR management.

Keywords: **Power BI, Attrition Analytics, Workforce Intelligence, HR Data Science, Predictive Retention Strategies, Employee Turnover.**

THE DYNAMIC LONG RUN AND SHORT RUN LINKAGES BETWEEN EXCHANGE RATES AND NSE NIFTY 50

Santhosh

MBA Research Scholar,
Soundarya Institute of Management Science

Yashaswini A

MBA Research Scholar,
Soundarya Institute of Management Science

Prof. Vaibhav S Arwade

Assistant Professor Department of MBA,
Soundarya Institute of Management Science
Email: vaibhavarwade@soundaryainstitutions.in

ABSTRACT

This study examines how exchange rate movements are connected to the performance of the NSE Nifty 50 index from January 2015 to November 2024. It looks at both the long-term and short-term relationships and how currency fluctuations affect stock market returns. To analyse this, we used various methods, including the **Augmented Dickey-Fuller (ADF)** test to check if the data is stable, correlation analysis to measure relationships, the **Vector Autoregressive (VAR)** model to study short-term effects, and the **GARCH model** to assess volatility. The results show that exchange rates and Nifty 50 returns are closely linked, often with a negative relationship. Exchange rate changes influence the stock market in the short term, and their volatility has a significant impact on market performance. This highlights the dynamic nature of the relationship between currency movements and stock market trends. The study emphasizes that investors should pay close attention to currency fluctuations, as they can pose risks to stock market investments. It also suggests that policymakers focus on strategies to stabilize exchange rates, as this can help reduce market uncertainty and support economic growth.

Keywords: Exchange Rates, NSE Nifty 50, Stock Market Volatility, VAR Model, GARCH Model, Correlation Analysis.

BITCOIN, BLOCKCHAIN, AND BEYOND: THE EVOLUTION OF DIGITAL CURRENCIES

Aaina Jain

MBA research Scholars
M/s Soundarya Institute of Management and Science, Bangalore-560073
Jainaaina82@gmail.com

Chethan G

MBA research Scholars
M/s Soundarya Institute of Management and Science, Bangalore-560073
gowdachethu83@gmail.com

Dr. Ramesh D

(Assistant Professor, Department of MBA)
M/s Soundarya Institute of Management and Science, Bangalore-560073 ramesh.may1981@gmail.com

ABSTRACT

The advent of Bitcoin and blockchain technology has revolutionized the financial landscape, introducing a decentralized and thrustless system of digital transactions. This research paper explores the evolution of digital currencies, tracing their origins from Bitcoin's inception to the development of alternative cryptocurrencies and decentralized financial applications. The study examines the fundamental principles of blockchain technology, including its security mechanisms, consensus protocols, and potential for financial inclusion. Furthermore, it analyzes the economic, regulatory, and technological challenges associated with cryptocurrency adoption, addressing concerns such as volatility, scalability, and regulatory uncertainty. Through a comprehensive review of existing literature and market trends, this paper evaluates the future trajectory of digital currencies and their impact on global financial systems. The findings highlight both the transformative potential and the limitations of cryptocurrencies in fostering a more decentralized, efficient, and accessible financial ecosystem.

Keywords: Bitcoin, Blockchain, Digital Currencies, cryptocurrency, financial.

ADVANCING DIVERSITY, EQUITY AND INCLUSION (DEI) IN THE WORKPLACE: STRATEGIES, CHALLENGES, AND BUSINESS IMPACT

Ms. Thanuja M

MBA Research Scholar,
Soundarya Institute of Management Science

Ms. Nageshwari k

MBA Research Scholar,
Soundarya Institute of Management Science

Dr. Roopa Shettigar

Associate Professor, Department of MBA,
Soundarya Institute of Management and Science
roopashettigar@soundaryainstitutions.in

ABSTRACT

In today's corporate landscape, Diversity, Equity, and Inclusion (DEI) have emerged as crucial elements that drive innovation, boost employee engagement, and enhance overall business performance. A workforce comprising diverse individuals brings a range of viewpoints, stimulating creativity and enhancing problem-solving capabilities. Equity ensures that all employees are given fair chances, while inclusivity creates an environment where staff members feel valued, respected, and empowered. Studies show that companies with robust DEI practices witness increased employee productivity, enhanced innovation, and greater profitability. Nevertheless, implementing DEI initiatives comes with its own set of challenges, including unconscious bias, resistance to change, and difficulties in evaluating DEI effectiveness. To overcome these hurdles, organizations must employ data-driven strategies, secure leadership buy-in, establish fair recruitment processes, and offer ongoing DEI training. This study examines key approaches for advancing DEI, identifies common obstacles faced by organizations, and assesses the long-term business impact of cultivating an inclusive work environment. Future research should concentrate on enhancing DEI measurement frameworks and identifying industry-specific best practices for maintaining diversity, equity, and inclusion.

Keywords: Diversity, Equity, Inclusion, Workplace Culture, Business Performance, HR Strategies.

THE EVOLUTION AND IMPACT OF DIGITAL MARKETING IN THE MODERN BUSINESS LANDSCAPE

Shobhitha R

MBA Research Scholar , Soundarya Institute of
Management Science
Email: shobithar91@gmail.com

Rakshitha M R

MBA Research Scholar, Soundarya Institute of
Management Science
Email: rg533808@gmail.com

Prof. Shareef A P

Assistant Professor, Department of MBA
Soundarya Institute of Management Science
Email: shareef.ap@soundaryainstitutions.in

ABSTRACT

Digital marketing has transformed the way businesses connect with consumers by utilizing digital channels to enhance brand awareness, customer engagement, and sales conversions. With the rapid evolution of technology, businesses have shifted from traditional marketing methods to data-driven digital strategies that leverage platforms such as social media, search engines, email marketing, and content marketing. This paper examines the fundamental components of digital marketing, including search engine optimization (SEO), pay-per-click (PPC) advertising, social media marketing, influencer marketing, and data analytics. It also explores the role of artificial intelligence (AI), machine learning, and automation in optimizing marketing campaigns and improving customer experiences.Furthermore, this study analyses the impact of digital marketing on consumer behaviour, emphasizing personalization, targeted advertising, and user engagement. While digital marketing offers numerous advantages, including cost-effectiveness and global reach, businesses face challenges such as data privacy concerns, algorithm updates, online competition, and ad fatigue. The paper also highlights emerging trends such as voice search optimization, interactive content, and omnichannel marketing strategies, which are shaping the future of the industry. By evaluating current trends and future projections, this research underscores the necessity for businesses to adopt innovative, data-driven approaches to remain competitive in the digital landscape. The findings suggest that integrating AI-powered tools, leveraging big data analytics, and prioritizing customer-centric marketing strategies will be key to achieving long-term success. Ultimately, businesses that embrace digital transformation and continuously adapt to changing consumer preferences will gain a significant competitive advantage in the evolving digital marketplace

Key words: Digital marketing, search engine optimization (SEO), social media marketing, content marketing, pay-per-click (PPC) advertising, influencer marketing, data analytics, artificial intelligence (AI), machine learning, automation, consumer behaviour.

THE IMPACT OF ARTIFICIAL INTELLIGENCE ON HR: AI, RECRUITMENT, TALENT MANAGEMENT AND EMPLOYEE ENGAGEMENT

Mamatha S M

MBA Research Scholar
Soundarya Institute of Management and Science
Email: smmamatha910@gmail.com

Varshini N B

MBA Research Scholar
Soundarya Institute of Management and Science
Email: varshinivarshanb@gmail.com

Prof. Shareef A P

Assistant professor
Department of MBA
Soundarya Institute of Management and Science
Email: shareef.ap@soundaryainstitutions.in

ABSTRACT

Artificial Intelligence (AI) is revolutionizing Human Resource Management (HRM) by enhancing efficiency, optimizing decision-making, and transforming employee experience. The adoption of AI in HR processes, such as recruitment, performance management, training, and employee engagement, has led to increased automation and data-driven insights. AI-powered algorithms facilitate resume screening, predictive analytics, and candidate matching, thereby reducing human biases and improving hiring outcomes. Additionally, AI-driven chatbots and virtual assistants streamline employee communication and HR service delivery, reducing administrative burden and enhancing workforce productivity. AI's influence extends to employee development through personalized learning platforms that analyze individual performance and recommend targeted upskilling initiatives. In talent retention, AI-driven sentiment analysis monitors employee feedback and predicts attrition risks, allowing HR managers to take proactive measures. Moreover, AI enhances workplace diversity and inclusion by identifying and mitigating unconscious biases in HR processes. Despite its benefits, AI adoption in HRM raises ethical and regulatory concerns, such as data privacy, transparency, and the potential for algorithmic bias. Organizations must implement AI responsibly, ensuring compliance with labor laws and ethical guidelines while maintaining a balance between automation and human oversight. Additionally, as AI automates repetitive HR tasks, the role of HR professionals is evolving, necessitating the acquisition of new skills to leverage AI-driven insights effectively. This paper explores the transformative impact of AI on HRM, analyzing its implications for workforce management, employee well-being, and organizational efficiency. The study highlights both the advantages and challenges associated with AI integration, providing insights into best practices for ethical AI implementation in HRM. The findings contribute to ongoing discussions on the future of work, emphasizing the need for HR professionals to embrace AI while maintaining a human-centric approach to workforce management.

Keywords: Artificial Intelligence, Human Resource Management, Recruitment Automation, Talent Analytics, Workforce Productivity.

THE IMPACT OF ESG REPORTING ON PERFORMANCE: INSIGHTS FROM THE INDIAN BANKING SECTOR

Nayana B

Student MBA Final Year,
Soundarya Institute of Management and Science, Bengaluru.

Nisha K M

Student MBA Final Year,
Soundarya Institute of Management and Science, Bengaluru.

Prof. Vaibhav S Arwade

Assistant Professor Department of MBA,
Soundarya Institute of Management Science
vaibhavarwade@soundaryainstitutions.in

ABSTRACT

Environmental, Social, and Governance (ESG) reporting has become a key factor in assessing corporate performance and stakeholder trust. This study examines the impact of ESG reporting on the financial performance of Indian banks, focusing on 30 listed banks from 2015 to 2023. Key performance indicators analyzed include return on assets (ROA), return on equity (ROE), and non-performing assets (NPA). Data were collected from secondary sources such as bank websites, sustainability reports, and the Reserve Bank of India (RBI) database. The study employs panel regression models, correlation analysis, and Granger causality tests to evaluate the relationship between ESG reporting and financial performance. The results indicate a significant positive correlation between ESG disclosure scores and financial performance, with banks demonstrating strong ESG frameworks exhibiting higher profitability and lower NPA ratios.The findings highlight the growing importance of ESG integration in corporate governance, emphasizing its role in risk management and investor confidence. This study contributes to the literature on sustainable banking practices in emerging economies and provides insights for policymakers, investors, and financial institutions. It underscores the need for Indian banks to enhance ESG disclosures to achieve long-term financial stability and a competitive edge. Future research can explore qualitative factors such as management perception and customer sentiment toward ESG initiatives.

Keywords: ESG reporting, financial performance, Indian banking sector, panel regression, sustainability, corporate governance.

THE ROLE OF PRIVATE EQUITY IN INDIAN AVIATION

Professor Prema Venkatraman

Program In Charge – BBA Aviation
Department of Business Administration
prema@soundaryainstitutions.in

ABSTRACT

The aviation industry, characterized by high capital requirements, cyclical demand, and stringent regulatory oversight, has increasingly attracted the attention of Private Equity Firms. This research paper explores the role of Private Equity in Aviation, examining how Private Equity investments have influenced the industry's growth, operations, and competitive landscapes. The paper delves into the motivations behind private equity investments, the types of aviation sectors targeted, and the implications for stakeholders including airlines, manufacturers, service providers and consumers.

Key Words : Private Equity , Aviation Investment Strategies , Regulatory Oversight , Competitive Landscape.

REVOLUTIONIZING PERFORMANCE MANAGEMENT: STRATEGIES FOR EMPLOYEE GROWTH AND ENGAGEMENT

Vaishnavi G

MBA Research Scholars
Soundarya Institute of Management and Science, Bangalore -560073
vaishnavigopinath03@gmail.com

Teja Babu KP

MBA Research Scholars
Soundarya Institute of Management and Science, Bangalore -560073
tejuteja082@gmail.com

Angel Chakraborty

Assistant Professor, Department of MBA
Soundarya Institute of Management and Science, Bangalore -560073
angel.chakraborty@soundaryainstitution.in

ABSTRACT

As businesses evolve, traditional performance management is shifting toward innovative, employee-centric approaches that foster talent development, engagement, and productivity. Annual appraisals are being replaced by continuous feedback, AI-driven analytics, skill-based assessments, and personalized development plans, ensuring real-time insights, goal alignment, and career progression. This study explores emerging trends such as agile performance management, 360-degree feedback, OKRs, and AI-powered coaching, which enhance employee growth and strategic alignment. Additionally, data-driven decision-making, gamification, and behavioral analytics are transforming performance measurement and improvement. By adopting these modern performance management strategies, businesses can build a high-performance culture that emphasizes learning, adaptability, and employee well-being. The research provides insights into best practices, challenges, and implementation frameworks, highlighting performance management as a strategic tool for long-term talent development and organizational success.

Keywords: Innovative performance management, talent development, continuous feedback, AI-driven analytics, employee engagement, skill-based assessment, OKRs, 360-degree feedback, gamification, high-performance culture.

AI-DRIVEN TALENT ACQUISITION: ENHANCING RECRUITMENT EFFICIENCY AND MITIGATING BIAS IN HIRING

Reshmi Raj K V

MBA Research Scholars
Soundarya Institute of Management and Science, Bangalore -560073
reshmibaburaj783@gmail.com

Varshitha H S

MBA Research Scholars
Soundarya Institute of Management and Science, Bangalore -560073
varshithahs626@gmail.com

G Vasanth Kumar

Assistant Professor, Department of MBA
Soundarya Institute of Management and Science, Bangalore -560073
mail id: vasanthkumar.g@soundaryainstitutions.in

Abstract

Artificial Intelligence (AI) is transforming talent acquisition by enhancing efficiency, improving candidate selection, and mitigating bias in hiring. Traditional recruitment often suffers from unconscious biases, leading to reduced workforce diversity. AI-driven recruitment, leveraging machine learning and natural language processing, aims to create a more objective and data-driven hiring process. This study analyzes the impact of AI in bias reduction through a quantitative assessment of 200 recruitment cycles across various industries. Results indicate a 27% improvement in candidate-job match accuracy and a 35% increase in diversity hiring rates. Furthermore, bias detection algorithms flagged 18% fewer discriminatory patterns compared to traditional methods ($p < 0.05$). However, challenges remain, as AI systems trained on biased historical data still exhibited a 12% disparity in gender-based recommendations ($p = 0.03$) (Smith & Lee, 2023). Regulatory frameworks and ethical considerations are crucial to ensuring unbiased AI adoption in recruitment (Johnson, 2024). By evaluating AI's role in talent acquisition, this research contributes to HR technology innovation and guides organizations toward ethical, high-performing hiring strategies.

Keywords: AI-driven recruitment, talent acquisition, hiring bias, workforce diversity, machine learning in HR, ethical AI, HR analytics, bias mitigation.

THE INFLUENCE OF WORK-LIFE BALANCE ON EMPLOYEE RETENTION

Yashaswini A

Student final year MBA,
Soundarya Institute of Management and Science, Bengaluru.

Santhosh

Student final year MBA,
Soundarya Institute of Management and Science, Bengaluru.

Prof. Vaibhav S Arwade

Assistant Professor Department of MBA,
Soundarya Institute of Management Science
vaibhavarwade@soundaryainstitutions.in

ABSTRACT

Work-life balance (WLB) has emerged as a critical factor influencing employee retention in modern organizations. This study examines the relationship between work-life balance and employee retention, focusing on how flexible work arrangements, workload management, and organizational support contribute to employees' decision to stay with their employer. A quantitative research approach was adopted, collecting data from **300 employees** across various industries using a structured questionnaire. The study utilized **Likert-scale responses** to measure employees' perceptions of work-life balance and their intention to remain in their current jobs. Statistical analysis was conducted using **SPSS**, employing **descriptive statistics, correlation analysis, and multiple regression** to determine the strength and significance of the relationship between WLB and retention. The results indicate a **strong positive correlation ($r = 0.72$, $p < 0.01$)** between work-life balance and employee retention. Employees who reported higher satisfaction with work-life balance were significantly more likely to stay with their organizations. **Flexible work hours and remote work options emerged as key predictors** of retention, while excessive workload and lack of organizational support were major factors contributing to turnover intentions. These findings highlight the importance of HR policies that promote work-life balance to enhance employee satisfaction and reduce attrition rates. Organizations should implement flexible work arrangements and supportive policies to improve retention and overall workplace well-being.

Keywords: Work-life balance, Employee retention, Flexible work arrangements, Organizational support, Turnover intentions, HR policies, Job satisfaction.

A STUDY ON THE IMPACT OF MODERN MARKETING STRATEGIES ON THE SUCCESS OF NEW PRODUCTS

Revathi.M

PhD Research Scholar (Part-Time)
Rvs College Of Arts and Science
Sulur, Coimbatore.

Dr.K.Sarulatha

Assistant Professor
School of Business Management
RVS College of Arts and Science
Sulur, Coimbatore

ABSTRACT

Modern marketing methods have changed to take use of innovative technologies and innovative strategies in the current digital world. These tactics cover a broad spectrum, such as influencer collaborations, content marketing, social media interaction, data-driven marketing, and search engine optimization (SEO). Businesses may better target certain consumers with their marketing campaigns by utilizing big data and analytics. The environment has also changed as a result of the growth of mobile marketing and customized customer experiences, which enables businesses to communicate with customers instantly. All things considered, contemporary marketing tactics emphasize developing deep, tailored connections that increase engagement and cultivate brand loyalty. The purpose of this study is to examine at the significance modern methods of marketing are to a new product's success. The potential impact of contemporary marketing techniques, such as influencer, content, loyalty, social media, and targeted email campaigns, on increasing the success rate of new goods is evaluated. The goal of the study is to show how a new product's overall performance is correlated with the use of various contemporary marketing strategies.

DIGITAL PAYMENT SYSTEMS: IMPACT ON CONSUMER SPENDING BEHAVIOUR

Tanvi Kurtiker

Assistant Professor, Department of Economics,
Dnyanprassarak Mandal's College and Research Centre, Assagao-Goa.

Danica F. Menezes

Assistant Professor, Department of Economics
Dnyanprassarak Mandal's College and Research Centre, Assagao-Goa.

ABSTRACT

Increased adoption of digital payment systems in current times has transformed consumer spending behavior significantly changing the traditional purchasing patterns. The present study tries to explore the impact of digital payment methods among the young crowd. The paper tries to examine the psychological and economic implications of cashless transactions, analyzing consumption and the possible challenges associated with the same. Additionally, it investigates demographic and social differences in adoption of digital payment methods. Methodology to be adopted for the study is non probability sampling technique and the data collection tool for the same is structured questionnaire and interview.

Key Words : Digital Payments, Cashless Transactions, Psychological andEconomic Implications.

LEADERSHIP IN REMOTE WORK MODELS: SHAPING THE FUTURE OF WORK FOR A DIGITAL ERA

Amruta V Chougule

Research scholar, Department of Management Studies,
Visvesvaraya Technological University, Belagavi

Dr. Sandhya Anvekar

Professor, Department of Management Studies,
Visvesvaraya Technological University, Belagavi

ABSTRACT

The shift toward remote work has revolutionized traditional leadership strategies and created an urgent need for innovative distributed team leadership methods and organizational performance maintenance systems. Researchers aim to analyse how leadership functions in remote work platforms their effects on workplace transformations. Research seeks to determine successful leadership approaches in remote environments while examining leadership challenges and remote work advantages and measuring its lasting impact on worker engagement and company performance and team organizational culture. This research investigates remote work success through case studies of implementing organizations while conducting surveys that include leaders and employees from various sectors. Proofs about virtual leadership excellence come from structured interviews and employee feedback reviews and quantitative performance measurements. The research shows transformational and servant leadership practices excel in virtual settings which focus on building trust alongside digital collaboration and strong communication practices. The analysis indicates several essential remote work difficulties concerning employee retention and fair career development and remote worker stress management. The analysis shows how technology-based leadership systems that incorporate AI tracking data and virtual communication tools will reshape future work environments. Organizations need to create leadership development programs matching remote and hybrid models while developing leader digital literacy and maintaining employee wellness for building long-term high-performing remote teams. The research findings enhance the ongoing dialogue about adaptive leadership in digital times through actionable guidelines that help companies direct their future workplace development.

About **Soundarya Institute of Management and Science (SIMS), Bengaluru**

Soundarya Institute of Management and Science (SIMS), Bengaluru, is a prestigious educational institution offering a wide range of undergraduate and postgraduate programs in management, commerce, and science. Established in 2007 with just 92 students, SIMS has grown significantly and now accommodates over 1500 students. The institute is committed to academic excellence, providing a dynamic learning environment that integrates theoretical knowledge with practical skills. With a distinguished faculty, cutting-edge infrastructure, and a curriculum tailored to industry demands, SIMS emphasizes research, innovation, and collaboration with industries. This approach ensures students are equipped to thrive in the global business landscape. Through its student-centric focus, SIMS continues to nurture future professionals capable of tackling the challenges of tomorrow.

ABOUT DEPARTMENT OF MBA

MBA Department – Soundarya Institute of Management and Science, Bangalore

The MBA program at **Soundarya Institute of Management and Science (SIMS), Bangalore,** is dedicated to shaping globally competent and industry-ready management professionals. The curriculum emphasizes research, practical learning, and global exposure, providing students with essential skills to thrive in a competitive business environment. At SIMS, students engage in research across diverse fields such as finance, marketing, and human resources, earning accolades and awards at prestigious conferences. The **Global Immersion Program** offers academic and industry visits to Singapore and Malaysia, enriching students' understanding of cross-cultural business practices. To bridge the gap between academic knowledge and industry requirements, **"Embark Sessions"** with industry leaders and top academicians, including experts from the **IIMs,** are held regularly. Additionally, students gain proficiency in tools like **Power BI, SPSS, Python,** and **R,** preparing them for advanced roles in analytics, financial modeling, and predictive analysis. SIMS ensures that MBA graduates are research-driven, globally exposed, and technologically empowered.